DON'T RUB 'EM, COUNT 'EM

DON'T RUB 'EM, COUNT 'EM

JOHNNY RAY

Matador
Unit E2 Airfield Business Park,
Harrison Road, Market Harborough,
Leicestershire. LE16 7WB
Tel: 0116 2792299
Email: books@troubador.co.uk
Web: www.troubador.co.uk/matador
Twitter: @matadorbooks

ISBN 978 1803130 019

British Library Cataloguing in Publication Data.
A catalogue record for this book is available from the British Library.

Printed and bound in Great Britain by 4edge Limited
Typeset in 12pt Adobe Jenson Pro by Troubador Publishing Ltd, Leicester, UK

Matador is an imprint of Troubador Publishing Ltd

In memory in part to Micky Eason (1943-2020)

JUST A TASTER FOR WHAT IS TO COME

'Two flies playing football in a saucer – One fly says to the other fly, "We've got to play better than this next week, we're playing in the cup."

—

Two old boys in their 80s Joe & George, were reminiscing about their times spent together playing and watching football. Joe wasn't at all well, in fact he was pretty much on his last legs.

George said to Joe, "When you pass on and go to heaven do me a favour and let me know if there's football up there, if so it won't worry me so much about dying myself.

Shortly after, poor old Joe does die and leaves George on his own. A little while later, George was asleep in bed when he was awakened by a flash of white light and a voice. George said "Who is it?" The voice replied, " It's Joe George and I 've got some good and bad news about the football up here, what do you want first?" George replied "The good first," so Joe said "Well, there is football up here and all our friends that have died over the years have reverted back to their youth and are playing it." To which George says, "Oh good" and asks "What's the bad news?"

To which Joe replies "Your name's on the team sheet for Saturday."

There was a football match between the insects and the animals and half-time the animals were leading 5-0. In the second half the insects brought their sub on a centipede in the 75th minute and he scored five goals to make the final score 5-5.

At the final whistle, the manager of the animals said to the manager of the insects "Why didn't you bring him on earlier, you probably would have gone on to win the game" with the manager of the insects replying, "We told him he was going on at half – time but it took him 30 minutes to put his boots on."

—

A coach driver takes a coach load of blind kiddies out on a day trip.

The driver decides that he takes a lunchbreak and pulls up outside a country pub with a large green outside of it, pulling from underneath his driver's seat a football with a bell in it

He tells the boys that he's going in the pub to have his lunch for an hour and that they should take the ball and go on the green and have a game of football.

After about 20mins. he's sitting at the bar when a lady from the village enters the pub shouting "Who's responsible for those boys out on the green?" To which the driver admits he is why?

The lady says "Well you'd better get out there quick as they're kicking shite out of the Morris Dancers."

INTRO

This is an anecdotal book of stories and tails, written by a working class boy who was brought up by working class parents half a mile from Tottenham Hotspur's White Hart Lane ground, parents that were extremely loving and of high moral standards, along with 'other famous' people although not necessarily by working class parents, the likes of the singers Adele, Lemar and Dave Clark of the Dave Clark Five, the actors Ron Moody, Leslie Phillips and Frances de la Tour (albeit not sure about the latter), Sue Gray, who's been appointed to carry out the Conservative Government's coronavirus 'Partygate' debacle and Julius Caesar, no not him, the 16th century judge (Google it).

That said, he would always tell people that he did play at a reasonably high level, "Half way up Mount Kilimanjaro" and that "You couldn't take a beach ball off him in a phonebox." Neither of which were true, although he'd like to think that the latter was, although he was once compared to Glen Hoddle with someone saying, "Compared to Glen Hoddle you're shite."

That said, he did kick his first football when he was physically able to and his last when he was 72, albeit playing 'Walking Football.'

As a very young lad, he couldn't wait for the paper boy to deliver his CHARLIE BUCHAN's FOOTBALL MONTHLY or his weekly TIGER comic, that featured his and every other kiddie's idol at the time Roy Of The Rovers, the Harry Kane of his time.

He remembers when Roy's club Melchester Rovers, went on a pre-season tour to South America and on their way to training they witnessed a bank robbery. Roy took one of the balls out of the sack that they were in, jumped from the coach that they were travelling in and kicked it at the getaway car's windscreen to smash it, which enabled the police to arrest the 'bandits involved,

Ridiculous, but he probably believed it at the time.

Being poor is all relative but his parents could only afford the basic essentials, with having to make do with things that could deputise for the real thing, like using the Readers Digest for shin pads. He didn't get on with those 'nailed on' wooden studs on those '1950s Stanley Matthews 'oh so cumfy boots' either, the ones with the almost steel toe cap, in fact his dad used to take the studs out and replace them with strips of leather placed at even intervals across the sole of the boot. He'd like to see David Beckham score from the half way line as he did against Wimbledon in 1996 or Lionel Messi do his stuff with them on, mind you, you needed the toe cap to kick that bloody great leather ball that seemed to go hand in hand with the boots.

THE WARM UP

May I start by saying, that apart from my family, football has been pretty much my obsession in life, so much so that someone once said, if on my passing an autopsy was to be carried out on me and they opened up my skull, 'they' would probably find a deflated football rather than a brain, charming but possibly true.

I started to write this in around 1989, just before I, having lived in North London all my life, decided to move out to live in Norfolk with my wife and very young daughter so as to, as much as anything, give her a better way of life.

Because of our move, I put the book on hold not knowing if I'd ever resurrect it. About the same time, myself and a friend devised a football based board game. It was a question and answer game, the game board being similar to a Monopoly board with 'Home' and 'Away' squares placed alternately around the edge of it, the idea being that you could choose to answer 'draw' or 'win' questions for 1 or 3 points depending on what type of square you landed on after throwing a dice which was, incidentally, round like a football with a lead weight in it to prevent it from rolling too much which I acquired from a novelty/magic shop in Upper Street, Islington The questions were based on a degree of ease and difficulty e.g. the 'Home

Draw' questions would be relatively easy the 'Home Win' questions slightly harder, the 'Away Draw' questions harder still and the 'Away Win' questions being the most difficult, on a par with 'Penalty' square questions that were placed strategically around the board, similar in a way to 'Go To Jail' in Monopoly. There was also a league ladder inserted in the board, so that players of the game could move up and down the ladder depending on whether they got a question right or not.

We actually got to the stage where we put it in the hands of a marketing company to get it launched who advised us not to get a player who was currently playing for a team to endorse it, as people who supported other teams that 'he' didn't play for wouldn't buy it. On the basis of what the marketing company advised, we decided that we would approach 'Saint & Greavesie,'the one time Liverpool player Ian St. John & Jimmy Greaves who had the very popular TV programme at the time. On doing so 'their people' informed us that they'd only just put their name to a similar game that was being launched at Hamley's toys and games store in a few weeks time. I went to Hamley's in Holborn when they opened their doors at 9 a.m. on the day just to see what the game was like, only to find that it was similar but not as good as ours, well I would say that wouldn't I? Actually, we saw quite a few representatives of companies to try to get it marketed before we went with the company that we did, which made us think that our idea was stolen. In fact we even went to see the, as he was at the time, Spurs Chairman Irving Scholar in his office in Maddox Street just off of Regents Street to see if he was interested in investing in it, which unfortunately he wasn't . I'm not saying for one moment it was him who stole our idea mind. We had copyrighted the game and thought about taking the other company to court but it was explained to me by a games lawyer, that we'd both start off at £50 in costs, then a number of noughts would be added on to it and it would be the first one to run out of noughts that would lose the case, so that was the end of that.

What encouraged me to think about resurrecting this book, was what happened when I played in my last eleven a-side game at the age of 62 in 2006, a game that incidentally I was awarded 'Man of the Match' in by one of the organisers sons, for which I was extremely grateful.

It was an annual charity game on behalf of the owner of Easton Coach's daughter up here in Norfolk, who sadly died following a horse riding accident that she had. After the game as always every year, we went into The Unicorn pub in the market town of Aylsham where the game was played, not too far from Cromer where I now live for drinks and after match food. I was talking to one of the local lads who is known locally as 'Skid,' who I knew who also played in the game saying to him, "I haven't seen you playing for Alysham lately," which is the local team playing in the Anglian Combination League, to which he replied "Nah I'm too old, I'm thirty now" to which I replied "30? You're only a baby, you don't know what you're going to miss, not just the playing but all the fun and camaraderie that it can give you." After that, I thought to myself I must get my book 'off the ground' again and out of boredom of the coronavirus I did.

Incidentally 'Skid's' a good bloke, but he did try to tackle me out of that game, which he reminded me of just recently, that said, he has now relented and started playing 'vets' football so hopefully he took on board what I said.

When I was younger around Skid's age, most companies that you worked for had a football team, many of the companies with their own pitches and club houses and to that end, if you played for the company's team you still got paid if you got injured. I understand things are different nowadays, those days are gone, notwithstanding that it costs an 'arm and a leg' to get insured, if you can that is, especially if you're self-employed or on a zero contract.

I guess by writing this book, what I'm trying to say is, it's not just the professional game that's the 'be all and end all' of football.' It's out there for everybody to enjoy at varying levels whether it be playing, being in the dressing rooms, on the terraces, around the perimeters of Sunday morning park pitches or in the club houses or pubs after a game. The problem is the game is being made so divisive and although much of what I have written involves the professional side of the game, we should never forget the 'grass roots of football' where it all started from. What the wonderful game of football can give, whether it be by playing it or just watching can be equally enjoyable at every level.

In relation to the previous paragraph just for example, I'd like to pose the question. "Why is a cynical foul committed by a last defender on an attacker bearing down on goal, whereby the defender gets sent off, known as a professional foul? What's the difference in the foul being committed by a 'professional' player in front of 60k fans at say Old Trafford any different to the same foul committed by a 17 stone still drunk from the night before centre back over a local recreation ground week in week out?.

Also, the old adage 'Money Is The Root Of All Evil,' was never more profound than when it was associated with professional football and the Premier League. As an obsessive fan of this subjective and opinionated wonderful game, over the latter years I have become increasingly disheartened and disillusioned with it, especially with the extortionate amounts of money that players are being paid each week with, as it seems, 'good money being thrown at bad' as clubs search for the 'Holy Grail.'

The problem is, every club thinks it has a divine right to be successful and win trophies but the problem is, there aren't enough trophies to go round.

When I talk to others about the monies some footballers are being paid, they always come back with the old one, "It's all about supply and demand." Well I'll tell you what supply & demand is, it's a nurse who's been putting her life on the line by helping us all through the terrible coronavirus pandemic that's been going on as I write this, that's what supply & demand is and how much are they paid?

That said, I do understand that you can count the number of players that earn £200k a week on two hands and that by definition of their skills, it attracts the audiences and consequently the money to give TV companies, radio broadcasting companies such as Talksport and newspaper journalists their jobs but where's the justification in a footballer earning the same money in a week that the Prime Minister earns in a year.

Perhaps I'm being too idealistic but what I'd like to see, is some sort of 'performance related' salaries whereby players are paid according to their results but I won't hold my breathe.

Look at my club Tottenham Hotspur, as I write this book, the players have played eight games in twenty-one days just for the benefit of SKY and B.T. Sport to make them even wealthier than they are and on that subject, why do we need additional people other than a commentator to let us know what's going on in a game. Very often alongside the commentator, there is a summariser, the likes of Robbie Savage, Andy Hinchcliffe the one-time Man City full back and for it seems political correctness, a female to tell us what we've already seen and more often than not telling us what a player should have done with a ball when they never had the ability to do it themselves and then at half and full-time, they go back into the studio for another three or so analysers telling us what we've already seen and what they would have done if they'd been on the pitch, no wonder the TV subscriptions are so expensive to pay their salaries.

With regards to the aforementioned 'female' summariser, now I apologise if I'm coming over 'sexist' but female commentators just don't fit with me, they just don't sound right when commentating on men's football. Take the female who commentates on Match of the Day on Saturday nights, how come she always seems to get the last game on the programme when it's very often a 0-0 draw between two of the lower teams in the Premier League, how do the producers know its going to be a dour 0-0? You see, they only seem to include her to be it seems politically correct.

Over the last two weeks as I'm writing this, we've had the fans demonstrating against the forming of the European Super league by the so-called big six. I find this a little hypocritical, as the City fans couldn't wait to welcome the Saudis to invest their money into their club to make them successful in recent years, the Liverpool fans getting the Americans in so that they could buy arguably the best centre-back in the world to help them win the Champions League and the Chelsea fans getting Abramovich to help them be relatively successful over a period of time. And now, the United fans invading Old Trafford to show their disapproval of the Glazers ownership of the club. Why is it the fans approved of them investing their millions into the club to buy the likes of Pogba & Bruno Fernandes and now that the owners want to do what they want to with the clubs/businesses that they've bought, the fans don't like it, albeit in United's case I think it's more like the fans are jealous of what City have achieved in recent years with their investors.

n.b. You will no doubt notice, that I've not included Arsenal or Tottenham fans in this as they've not been as successful as the other four and if it hadn't have been for the wonderful stadium that Levy & ENIC have built for the club, Tottenham may have not been included as one of those 'top-six' clubs.

With these protestations, it seems to me that 'the worm is turning' and the fans, having been 'imprisoned' in their homes and having not been allowed to go to games over the past year due to the covid pandemic have been able to sit back and take stock and have now realised that they have been 'mugged off' and they're now fighting back albeit somewhat in an unruly fashion, which made many presenters especially on Talksport say that the fans should have protested in a more peaceful manner e.g. not go to the games. Really? The Glazers have got the money for the season tickets they wouldn't have cared less. On the subject of Talksport & SKY, they've both accused the six English clubs who were instrumental in wanting to form the Super League of being 'greedy' and not caring about the fans, well they've both got some front, what with Talskport charging up to 25p a minute to contact them to put your views on air and for SKY, with their extortionate subscription rates and with the way they go about re-scheduling games at the last minute to inconvenient times for especially travelling fans to get to, not withstanding that the travelling away fans had already lost money by having hotels and train fares booked for the originally scheduled game.

Also, the way the game is constantly changing is annoying, both in terms of competition formats such as the proposed European Super League and rule changes. It seems the 'people' in their ivory towers who supposedly run the game, have to be seen to be doing something just to justify their extortionate salaries they are receiving all coming out of the fans pockets. There doesn't seem to be any contentment or stability anymore, not just in football but in life in general. Take the 'rule changes' over recent years, o.k., some that have been brought into play have been good for the game e.g. The ball not having to go out of the penalty area from a goal kick, or the ball being given back to the team in possession when it hits the referee but God knows what having to pass back from the kick off is all about. Who came out with that one whilst sitting around a table at an all expenses paid dinner at a EUFA or FIFA meeting? Why can't 'they' come up with s sensible rule change e.g. when a player is fouled, sometimes badly enough for the opponent who committed the foul to be booked, the fouled player having to have treatment on the pitch then having to leave it whilst the ensuing free kick is taken with the fouled player's team being disadvantaged playing with 10 men? Where's the common sense in that?

Then we move onto VAR something we've actually had for many years 'Very Average Referees.' VAR's not a bad thing in itself, it seems to get more decisions right than wrong but it's only as good as the people operating it and even then they are governed and confused by the hierarchy making the rules for them to abide by. Why can't we go back to the dear old 'hand to ball' when it came to free kicks or penalties, or 'pure daylight' between the last defender and attacker with regards to offside, it would make things a lot more easier. In fact, what would make things easier is if we didn't have any 'action replays' at all like it was back in the day when there was nothing replayed to have a discussion or argument about, which would also overcome the 'too many summarising and analysing personnel' as mentioned in the previous paragraph so that the subscription costs to SKY and B.T. Sport could be reduced.

On a more radical note, because of the 'possession game' that the better teams can play these days, which at times can make parts of a game boring with the ball very often being played from front to back to the keeper, as is in the case of rugby, whereby a 'forward pass' is not aloud, why don't we do that in football ruling that backward passes are banned from being carried out at least in the team who has the ball's own half, that'd make it interesting when a centre back is chasing down an 'over the top ball' when facing his own goalkeeper.

Lucky I'm not in charge of the game eh?

Ostensibly, the book was to be solely about the anecdotal football stories that I've experienced over 70 or so years in the game, whether they be from playing, albeit at a comparatively low level as said, or from the banter and camaraderie either in the dressing rooms and in the clubhouses after a game, on the terraces and in the pubs before and after watching games. That said, I must admit, as I got deeper into writing the book it has turned out to be I suppose the memoirs of my life, at the same time keeping the book for the most part football orientated , so even if nobody buys it at least my daughter and grandchild will have something to remember me by and who knows, they might even be able to give copies out to those attending my cremation rather than those hymn sheets with a photo of me on them.

At this juncture, I'd like to apologise for any self indulgence that is written, especially much of it being written around my beloved Tottenham Hotspur, that said as someone has said to me, most books are written with an element of self-indulgence in them, whether it be an autobiography or even as a novel.

I have to say, at first I was reluctant to put this into print, as I thought it, for the most part being written around one club, fans of others wouldn't bother to read it, that said, Nick Hornby got away with writing 'Fever Pitch' as a Gooner, which made me think why not me, albeit I have to admit without the writing skills that he has been blessed with and with that in mind I'd just like to point out, that I haven't had the book 'proof read' as I wanted it to be written and worded to reflect if you like who and what I am, as described in the opening paragraph of the book.

Also, I have to admit, there is a small amount of 'journalistic license' in telling the stories and may I also apologise for any industrial language used, that said, football was based around the industrial society of the time so why not? In fact, it really annoys me in this current day and age, when television commentators have to apologise for any heard. If you don't like it turn the sound down as it all goes 'hand in hand' with the game

In conclusion, I hope you enjoy it, that said please persevere until you reach the '2nd Half,' as with most football matches the '2nd Half' is more entertaining and in this case funnier than the $1.^{st}$ Who knows, many of you may recognise places and people mentioned.

So here goes, the Ref's whistle has blown and if it's still happening at the time you read this, 'Take the knee' and we're off.

THE FIRST HALF

"Don't rub 'em count, 'em," as in the title of the book was the instruction bellowed by Don Keys to his PE teacher Dickie Moss having received a direct hit in the goolies from a shot from yours truly, Dickie, having come onto the pitch to attend to Don when he buckled under feeling the full blow of my shot.

This was the first comical situation happening on a pitch that I can recall, it being back in the '50s, I was coming up to 14 at the time, playing for my U-15 school team Parkhurst on Tottenham Marshes where our home pitch was situated.

I'd just parted company with Tottenham County School, which I left mutually, on the basis that the head teacher didn't think I was 'cut out' for the school in part because I didn't do my homework. I didn't want to go there anyway, I only did so because evidently, I'd done quite well in the first half of taking my A-Levels when I was at Coleraine Park Junior School, only not to complete the second half, as I'd broken my collar bone half way through it.

At Coleraine, my form teacher was a man by the name of Frank Rowe, he was the brother of Arthur Rowe the manager of the Spurs teams that were successful throughout the 50s with his 'push & run' type of football. Weirdly, Mr. Rowe didn't take the schools football team, that was done by a woman whose name I can't recall, although I do recall that we played in blue shirts with yellow sleeves, blue shorts and blue & yellow hooped socks. Frank did take us for cricket though and I remember him in the playground putting a tanner(sixpence) inside a chalked circle of 6 inches in diameter as to where he thought the line and length of the ball should be pitched when you bowled it and if you hit it, you would keep the money he'd placed in there as a reward.

Because our school's name was Coleraine, every Monday I used to look out for the Northern Irish team of the same name's results and all I wanted to do from a very early age being at the school was to be a professional footballer when I left. Mr Gray our head teacher, was the one who recommended that I should go to a 'Grammar School,' even though I didn't complete my A-Levels because of my injury. The two grammar schools that I had a choice of going to were either, Tottenham Grammar, based in White Hart Lane where a friend of mine Micky Grimsdell went, who was the grandson of Arthur Grimsdell who captained Spurs to their 1921 F.A. Cup win, or Tottenham County, which I decided on up behind The Green by Philip Lane, South Tottenham.

I only agreed to go there in respect of my parents who were quite proud of my achievements, me, I was prepared to go to Parkhurst, a secondary modern school where I knew I could continue to play football and represent Tottenham Boys which I had been doing whilst at Coleraine my junior school. I knew my chances of continuing to be picked for Tottenham Boys would be hampered by the fact that Tottenham County was a rugby union playing school, although whilst I was there, there were a couple of players that did turn professional at football, one being Jackie Burkett, the left back of West Ham who played in their 1965 European Cup Winners team, a team it seemed you could only be picked for if your surname began with the letter 'B,' as in

Bond, Burkett, Boyce Bovington &, Brabrook, oh by the way, the other lad being George De'Ath who turned out to be an Arsenal keeper. There were quite a lot of us who preferred football to rugby and when we had what was known as a 'field afternoon' to play rugby, instead of waiting for the coach to take us from the school up by Philip Lane which was in effect in South Tottenham, to our playing field in Queens Street which was in North Tottenham, we'd leave earlier and go by public transport either on a bus, or on a train from Bruce Grove to White Hart Lane station which was near to our playing field. We'd get there and play for an hour or so using the rugby posts as our football goal posts but we very often got the cane for doing so, as football seemed to be sacrosanct when it came to the curriculum of what the school taught.

It was about this time that I was supposed to appear on the game show 'Take Your Pick' hosted by Michael Miles. I don't know how it came about but I went with my mum to the ATV Studios at Wembley where they filmed it. A part of the qualification process, was that you had to answer questions on a subject of your choice and of course I chose football. I was only 12 or 13 but I sailed through the qualification round but on the night of the show I bottled it, I just couldn't face the cameras and made out I wasn't feeling well much to the annoyance of my mum.

Going back to my opening paragraph, Don Keys was a member of the, at the time, well known and respected Tottenham 'Keys' family, that for the most part lived in Lorenco Road close to White Hart Lane Station, an area that was locally known as 'Little Russia'. It was said that the police at the time, would only enter into the road in pairs because of its 'roughness.' It was also said, that doors were installed in the attics throughout all of the terraced houses in the road in the event the police raided a particular house to arrest somebody so that they could hotfoot it from a house at one end of the road through the roof spaces to the other to avoid being caught. The incident in the opening paragraph as said, was about me playing for Parkhurst against Don's Rowland Hill School, an all boys school based in Lordship Lane Tottenham. It was considered to be a 'rough old school' and for the want of a better word, intimidating if you were to play a schools football match there, the visitors wingers never being able to 'hug' the touchline as you would very often get tripped up by the over enthusiastic lads from the school watching the game from the touchline.

Dickie Moss was the head teacher of the school, a very highly respected man with the kids, mainly I think because he had long hair in a style of a mullet albeit with not too much on top. I was to fall foul of him many years later, when as a telephone engineer (more of that later), I 'pulled' one of his staff one Friday lunch time in the Antwerp Arms close to the Spurs ground where he used to take them for drinks, I assume in appreciation of their work throughout the week, me drinking with my BT mates. Judith her name was and he had high regard of the lady's beauty. I think he was quite jealous about it and said to me once in the pub, when he found out that I'd taken her out, "You're a jammy bastard Johnny Ray." In an endearing way of course Dickie was also a real character and very funny, who along with a Mr. Mackay, another Rowland Hill teacher, gave me my first opportunity of playing for Tottenham Boys.

The Antwerp Arms or 'The Annie' as it is endearingly known as, is situated adjacent to White Hart Lane cemetery and Bruce Castle Park given its name funny enough because there is a castle in it. Rumour has it that Robert The Bruce was once imprisoned there, I don't know if it's true though. The area, is the only part of Tottenham that can be described as gentrified with the aforementioned cemetery stretching for about a mile from White Hart Lane itself in the north to the park in the south. Weirdly, in all the years that I lived in Tottenham, not too far away from it and the times that I've re-visited, whether it be for matches or just to reminisce, I've never for some reason set foot in the cemetery. As many Spurs fans know, the pub closed some years ago with the owners Enterprise Inns, allegedly wanting to sell it so that it could be turned into flats, which was successfully opposed to by locals who frequented it. It re-opened in 2015 as a Community Pub with the help of amongst others, a long time friend of mine by the name of Chrissy Lane who lives close by to it who was instrumental in getting the £250k funds together for it to happen, some of the contributors being Tottenham F.C., David Lammy and as I understand it Garry Mabbutt.

Although a Gooner, Chrissy is a great guy and I've known him since we were both 15 when I used to go round his mother's flat in Northumberland Park where he would play me his amazing collection of Blues records that he would get from people he knew in Liverpool docks, with the records having been brought over by American seamen, records like Anna by Arthur Alexander and the original Twist & Shout by The Top Notes, long before The Beatles did cover versions of them on the Please Please Me LP . Thankfully, the pub is now up and running again and is a great match day venue. I don't think people that frequent it realise how much appreciation they owe Chrissy and his colleagues and the effort they put into re-opening it for their convenience. Actually, I enjoy the experience of going there so much, that even though I may not have a ticket for a home game, I go down with friends of mine in Norfolk who do have season tickets just so that I can be in hearing vicinity of the stadium and to watch a game on TV in the pub on a home match day and to see Chrissy and have a drink with him.

Actually whilst writing this and the 'coronavirus lockdown' being eased, I'm looking forward to going down there at the next earliest opportunity as Chrissy tells me, that within the grounds of the cemetery there is a large lake that he often takes a walk around with its own heron patrolling it, something I'd love to see

As said, I represented Tottenham Boys and I recall a comical situation when we were about to play a 'cup-game.' Unfortunately, our right back broke his leg playing in the previous game to it. We were a bit light at right back, in fact we didn't have a genuine replacement but we did have an abundance of centre halves. One of them was a friend of mine by the name of Del Vickery and I remember Dickie Moss saying to Del in training one Thursday evening, "Vickery, as you know, our right back has broken his leg and we do not have a direct replacement but we do have an abundance of centre halves and we think that you are the best of those suited to adapt to playing there." Del responded by saying "But sir, I've never played right back" to which Dickie replied "That's ok, just go along to White Hart Lane on Saturday and watch Tottenham's right back play against Newcastle and play just like him. So off Del went on the Saturday to queue up at around 11.30. as we all did, to get into the 'Boys Enclosure' which was situated on the first tier of the East Stand corner of the Park Lane end, for I think it was at the time 1s/3d. You had to get there early in those days with the crowds of around 70 thousand to make sure you could get in.

Tottenham got a hammering on the day losing 3-1, with Newcastle's left winger Bobby Mitchell scoring a hat-trick, who gave our right back, who was supposed to be marking him a real run around. On the following Monday evening when we were at a training session, the first thing Del said to Dickie Moss on his arrival was, "Sir, are you sure you want me to play like Tottenham's right back?" Dickie just kept schtum but do you know who that Tottenham right back was? None other than (Sir) Alf Ramsey, yes the same Alf Ramsey that in my mind was instrumental in the decline of English football by getting rid of conventional wingers and replacing them with Alan Ball and Martin Peters in order for England to win the '66 World Cup, which made many managers afterwards follow suit thinking it was the way to go.

What the English team and clubs were good at for generations before, was the good old wingers the likes of Stanley Matthews of Blackpool, Bolton's John Connelly & Bryan Douglas of Blackburn on the right and Tom Finney of Preston North End, Burnley's Brian Pilkington & Peter Thompson of Liverpool on the left who would race and 'jink' their way to the byeline to cross the ball for the likes of Nat Lofthouse of Bolton, Blackpool's Stan Mortenson, Tommy Taylor of Manchester United and even our own Bobby Smith of Tottenham to soar and 'bullet' a header into the top corner of the net, a spectacle hardly ever witnessed on a football pitch these days. In fact, in the 55 years since that World Cup victory, I think it's fair to say that you can count on two hands wingers that could be in the same envelope as those mentioned above, possibly United's Ryan Giggs &Stevie Coppell, Liverpool's Steve McManaman and Tottenham's Chrissie Waddle, David Ginola and Gareth Bale when he played on the left wing for Tottenham and more recently Traore of Wolves, a player that really excites me. I can't even include David Beckham in that category, as great as he was as a 'crosser' of a ball, he couldn't really beat a man at pace to do it. Most wingers now, if there are any are of the 'inverted' type which I don't see the benefit of at all.

So no 'orthodox' wingers, no players standing on the post to defend corners, a basic defensive ploy that we were all taught at school back in the day and no putting a man on the oppositions team playmaker to mark him out of the game, you don't see any of that happening anymore, it's as if the modern day coaches/ managers are trying to 're-invent the wheel.'

Tottenham Hotspur, the club that I was 'given' to support was on the basis that I was brought up from birth in Baronet Road, approximately half a mile from the White Hart Lane ground, running parallel with Lansdowne Road and Park Lane with it joining St. Pauls Road & Vicarage Road which is opposite the south-east corner of the stadium's Park Lane End.

I guess I was quite lucky and privileged being born where and when I was, it gave me the immense pleasure of seeing Spurs win the League twice within a decade, the first time in the early 50s and the second time culminating in us winning the double, in fact it was that decade that not only put the football club on it but it put TOTTENHAM as a place on the world wide map.

By living quite close to the ground, I and some friends in my road in the 50s would go to the Spurs ground on every opportunity, especially during school holidays to collect autographs. We would get to the main west stand entrance about 9 in the morning to get the players autographs as they turned up for training, as they did in those days (no Hotspur Way facilities then) and be there for when they came out. In between, we'd entertain ourselves by having a match in the concourse area between the main gates, which we used as one goal and the barriers/handrails at the foot of the steps leading up to the seating area of the West Stand at the other. We'd spend as much time as we could there getting autographs. I remember on one occasion Billy Nicholson, Ted Ditchburn & Eddie Baily, all members of the 50s teams turning up in a Ford car owned by Eddie, he being quite renown for his 'shooting at the hip' and his 'blue' language telling us all in no uncertain terms to "Fuck Off" when we approached them for their autographs. The three of them, Ted, Eddie & Bill didn't have to travel far, they all lived next to one another at the back of the ground very close to what is now the 'Billy Nick' pub in Commonwealth Road. I remember another incident involving Eddie's choice of language, which if I remember correctly involved Jimmy Greaves in his debut in a Spurs shirt. It was in a reserve team fixture against Plymouth

Argyle down at their Home Park ground in Devon, incidentally where as a kid, I saw Stanley Matthews play for Stoke City as my mum, dad and I used to go to Plymouth quite a bit to visit my dad's brother on what was then the old 'Devon Bell' steam train from Paddington Station. Eddie Baily was in charge of the reserve team on the night and by all accounts, he spent the whole of it 'effing' & 'blinding' at our young right winger Jimmy Oliver. Evidently, it was that bad with his swearing echoing around the almost empty stadium that Argyle lodged an official complaint with Tottenham Hotspur Football Club. Going back to Ted Ditchburn, just as an aside, in the latter part of his career he had a sports shop a couple of doors away from the what was then The Northumberland Arms before it became the 'Bill Nick,' a fine pub it was too, having a couple of well kept snooker tables at the rear of it, not the pole that the dancers/strippers use that it has now. Also another Spurs player of the time Len Duquemin, our centre forward of the 50s teams had a newsagents at the top of Northumberland Park where it meets the High Road. Incidentally, I did attend Len's wedding. I wasn't invited, I just went along with hundreds of other fans to St. Mary's Church at the top of Lansdowne Road where it meets the High Road, he got married on a Saturday morning and played for Tottenham against Chelsea at the Lane in the afternoon. Similar situations like that occurred around those times. I went to a 'book signing' at the Co-op, which was directly opposite the church that Len and his wife got married in, the Co-op, no longer being there following the riots in the High Road in 2011, it being burnt to the ground. It was a book-signing commemorating the Queens Coronation in 1953, all about events of that year, the 'Stanley Matthews' F.A. Cup Final as it was known being one of them, I still have the book autographed by Sir Stanley himself

Around this time, not only would we go to first team games at the Lane, the first one I recall being v Middlesboro when they had Ugolini in goal, the great Wilf Mannion and Delapenha & Fitzimons on the wings but we'd also go to 'reserve' team games almost every time they played at The Lane. We would very rarely actually watch them play, we used to go down below the Park Lane or Worcester Avenue stands and have a game of our own, only running up to the terraces to see who'd scored if a cheer went up. At this juncture, anyone remember the factory that used to make tin cans, it being situated under the Park Lane stand? Not many I bet.

In those days, if we ever did watch a reserve game you could always stand behind the goal that Spurs were attacking and walk to the other end at half time to stand behind the opponents goal that they were defending. I remember us playing Reading once, their left back being a real nasty piece of work kicking our right winger up in the air at every opportunity. On one occasion, I remember him giving away a corner right where we were standing just to the left of the goal and as his momentum took him to the wall surrounding the pitch where he conceded the corner, I ran behind Del Vickery, he of the earlier Alf Ramsey story, to put my hand in between his torso and left arm which he had in his pocket and shook my fist at the player shouting expletives at him whilst doing so. The player thought it was Del's arm and voice and proceeded to jump over the pitch side wall to get at Del to confront him only to be fortunately stopped by a patrolling policeman. These were in the days when a fella used to walk around the pitch every 15mins with the 1st teams 'away' score being held up on boards which was the only way of knowing an 'away' score on the day, no Talksport with a radio in your ear in those days...

Standing behind the goals and being so close to the players and officials, gave the opportunity of bantering with them. I remember the linesman, as they do before the start of a game and at half-time, checking the side netting and that behind the goal for any holes that there may have been which could have caused an issue if the ball went into the goal and through the netting thereby making it uncertain in the eyes of the officials as to whether an actual goal could have been construed as a goal kick. The linesman pulled up the net behind the goal to show a small hole when one of the wags with us shouted "Linesman, don't worry about that little hole at the back of the net we have trouble finding the big 'fucker' at the front." Also when a keeper of the opposition booted a goal kick straight out of play on the half way line. he duly put his hand up to offer his apologies, to which again a wag responded by saying "It's alright keeper, you don't have to put your hand up we know who did it."

Unfortunately, those days have gone, there are no 'reserve' fixtures played on the 1st team's pitch anymore where you could witness, as I did once, Alfie Stokes the reserve team's striker, pulling our goalkeeper John Hollowbread's shorts down to below his knees to reveal his naked backside, as he only had a jock strap on, when he duly converted a penalty that he was invited to take to make a score Spurs Reserves 10 Southampton Reserves 2. Spurs with the likes of Barry Aitchinson on the wing and Roy Hollis at centre forward at the time.

In those days in Baronet Road close to the ground where I lived, we used to have 'street' games between the lads in our street and lads from another street as you could, as there weren't many cars on the road then. For goal posts we'd use a lamppost and in the middle of the road we'd pile up bricks or as 'Ron Manager' used to say we'd use 'jumpers for goalposts.' Actually the games used to give the people living in the street a lot of enjoyment with them very often hanging out of their upstairs open sashed windows cheering us on.

Not having hardly any cars to contend with, it also lent itself to us playing cricket in the street. Baronet Road was in effect one road, albeit it a 90 degree right angular type of road, coming, for those that don't know it, down from Lansdowne Road and then doing a right angle for it to come out into St. Pauls Road which was off of Park Lane. On the corner on the kerb where the road 'right angled,' was conveniently situated an old gas lamp pole that was converted into an electric street light, the bottom base of it being green in colour and a metre or so high that we used as the 'wicket.' Because of the 'wicket' being conveniently situated how it was you could hit an 'off drive' along the part of the road that led up to Lansdowne Road and a 'hook shot' along the part of the road that led to St. Pauls Road and to the right of the wicket was Baronet Close where you could 'off cut' the ball, Baronet Close incidentally, having an alley way at the end of it where I used to go through to make the 10 minute walk to the Spurs ground from my house.

I actually lived in Baronet Road from almost the day that I was born, as I said previously about half a mile from the ground, having returned there from a hospital in St. Pancras where my mum gave birth to me. I did so until I was about 26 and when I learnt to drive, I used to rent a garage from a lady who had around a half a dozen to rent at the rear of her house in St. Pauls Road where it met Park Lane. When they first came to Tottenham, Cyril Knowles & Pat Jennings, having come from Middlesboro & Watford respectively lived 'in digs' in the lady's house and I very often used to see them come out of the house on their way to training when I used to pick up my car and we'd always greet each other with a nod or hello. Actually, I reminded Pat of this when I met him a couple of years ago at Hotspur Way, he was very impressed and I have to say grateful that I remembered it and brought it back to his attention.

I don't know really why I went to school. I and other kids who came from the same working class background that I did didn't think we'd go to learn anything so that it would help us get a job when we left, in fact jobs were 'two a penny' at the time, I went because my friends did and I suppose to prevent the Truant Officer coming round to our house to ask my parents why I wasn't at school and prevent them from being fined I suppose, although the other thing I did want to do is actually play for a football team i.e. the school's team that consequently gave me the opportunity of representing Tottenham Boys.

I wasn't a very attentive scholar and I couldn't wait to leave Parkhurst School at 15 when I was able to, after Tottenham County and I parted company, as I've said previously mutually 18 months earlier. All I was interested in doing was sport, obviously football moreso. I was still bitter that I'd almost lost any dream I had of being a professional footballer by going to Tottenham County School whereby they played rugby union. I just fell out of the 'loop' with football, not being able to continue to represent Tottenham Boys as I had done when I was at my junior school, you just had to play at every increasing age group up until you were old enough to get the opportunity of joining the youth set up of a professional club. What I was privileged to do at Parkhurst, was to be appointed House Captain by our House master to select and run our house team in the annual 'house football competition,' as by his own admission he, being an art teacher, knew nothing about football. The house teams were made up of the conventional, nothing imaginative Red, Green, Yellow and Blue colours, mine being Blue. We weren't blessed with the best selection of lads but we as a team won the competition much to the annoyance of 'Pecker' Jones the house master of the yellow team, who thought his house team were favourites for the trophy, he gaining the nickname 'Pecker' by definition of the size of his nose. Actually, most of our teachers were real characters especially our music teacher Mr. Wright, or 'Wrighty' as he was known endearingly by his pupils. If you 'let one go' (farted) in class, he'd say, "I can't tell you to stop it as you don't know what direction it's going in." Also, if he had to go to see the headmistress during a lesson, he'd tell us to get on with our work but if he heard talking when he got back to the classroom he'd say, "Right, hands up all those that were talking." About three would put their hands up, so he'd tell all those that hadn't put their hands up to go to the front of the class and get the cane for lying. On other occasions, he'd come back from going somewhere during a lesson and say again, all of those that were talking to put their hands up, so knowing what he'd done previously most of the class would put their hands up in admittance of them talking, only for him to make everyone go to the front of the class and get the cane, you'd never know how to take him. He did have his good side though. We were allowed to take our 78rpm vinyl records to the lessons which he would let us play on his pinky/red coloured Dansette Major record player that he had on his desk if we behaved ourselves, those being the likes of the original 'Blue Suede Shoes' by Carl Perkins, Bill Haley's 'Rock Around The Clock (which I actually saw Bill Haley do at the Tottenham Palace live many years later) and Elvis's early stuff like 'Don't & 'Heartbreak Hotel,' not the 'corny' Las Vegas stuff that he did later in his life just before he sadly died. This was around 1957 and I took the first 78s that I ever bought, both on the same Saturday morning from Saville's Record Shop in Bruce Grove in Tottenham, those being Paul Anka's 'Diana' and Buddy Holly & The Crickets 'That'll Be The Day.' Talking about Carl Perkins's Blue Suede Shoes, do you know why the 'Wurlitzer Juke Box' popular throughout the 50's & 60's was called what it was? 'Wurlitzer one for the money, two for the show, three to get ready now go cat go.'

Reverting to 'Pecker Jones' the head of Yellow House, he really had it in for me at every opportunity afterwards because I was captain of Blue House that won the tournament that he thought he would win. Being a house captain, I was also appointed a Prefect, a position you were supposedly privileged in receiving in order that you ensured your fellow classmates and friends towed the school rules. On one really hot day, it being back in the 50s when summers were hot and winters freezing cold, I was on what was known as 'Gate Duty.' Doing this duty, one of the things you were responsible for was to prevent other kids from buying an ice-cream from a vendor who used to park outside the school gate after a certain bell was rung. Two bells used to ring at the end of lunch time, one at 1.20p.m. almost as a warning, for the next at 1.30 when we would all have to stand to attention before going off to our respective classes. The gate monitors duty was to not let anyone buy an ice-cream from the vendor after the first bell but on one occasion, a friend of mine who I played with in the schools team, the goalkeeper John Davies a tall lad, came running up to me whilst I was standing by the vendors van begging me to let him buy an ice-cream but I couldn't, because the first bell had sounded. I probably would have relented but the problem was, the schools headmistress's office was right above the school playground and gates and could see everything that was going on. I have to say that I wasn't that enamoured about being a Prefect, I never towed the line enough myself to warrant it really and it wouldn't have bothered me that much if my badge had been taken away from me but I was proud of the fact that I was a house captain and winning the 'house football trophy' especially against all the odds which brought me the position of being a Prefect. My friend continued to harass me as to letting him buy an ice-cream but I stood my ground but subconsciously, I worked my way to being between him and the ice-cream vendor only for the said vendor to hold up a nine inch blade which he had been using to slice up the ice-cream with to my throat, pulling my hair back with his free hand. He threatened me with the words "If you take my business away from me, I'll slit your throat you little bastard" but then thankfully letting me go. As you can imagine I was shaking like a leaf and went back to my classroom where 'Pecker Jones' was to take us for a geography lesson. After about 10 minutes there was a knock at the classroom door. 'Pecker' went over and opened it to find another Prefect there who told him that the Headmistress wished to see me. 'Pecker' asked what I'd been up to 'now' but I just ignored him, so he said "OK, I suppose you'd better get up there then." I knocked on the door and entered to find the Headmistress, Deputy Head and another senior teacher being in there with the Headmistress saying "We saw what happened down there, do you want us to call the police and press charges?

In anger I replied, "Hang on a minute, are you saying you all witnessed what happened and not one of you had the guts to come down to help? Well you can all fuck off" and I stormed out and went home. I was never punished out of, I should imagine embarrassment on their part albeit the ice-cream vendor got his through my dad, which I won't go into in detail except to say, that my dad could look after himself, being born in the late 1800s in Stepney in the heart of the East End of London doing a bit of bare-knuckle fighting in fairground arcades and fighting in the 1st World War and being a decent footballer himself playing left back for Clapton Orient in the 20s/30s who were a highly respected East London team at the time. My dad used to come to watch me play as much as he could when I was young and I remember him watching me play once standing on the touchline where I was playing on the left wing. Every time I went to go past the right back who was marking me, which was quite often, he was getting so frustrated he was kicking me all over the place with the referee not giving me much protection. My dad really took umbrage to this and took off his wellington boot and run onto the pitch to start hitting the full back with it, it was so embarrassing.

My dad never did speak to me much about the war, too many bad memories I guess, the only story I do remember him telling me was that he and his regiment were sitting around a fire where they were somewhere in India, when some massive snake indigenous to Asia, came into where they were camping and they had to turn the fire that they had made to keep them warm over onto the snake to kill it. Talking of camping, my Grandad was killed at The Battle of the Little Bighorn. He wasn't actually involved in the fighting but he was camping nearby and he only went over to complain about the noise (Only kidding).

My aunt Dolly did tell me once that my dad's regiment's patrol, when walking through France on their way back to England, were chased down by German troops many of them in vehicles. When they heard them coming, my dad's regiment ran from the roads to hide in the surrounding fields but his brother, who was in the same regiment, decided to hide in a hay cart. By all accounts my dad witnessed his brother being stabbed to death by a bayonet wielding German. My dad evidently tried to break ranks and run to help his brother only fortunately for his colleagues to hold him down, which I assumed he was grateful for as he lived to 92 years of age. My aunt Dolly also told me that my dad used to live with her in Asplins Road in Tottenham and he used to have a horse and cart to sell fruit & veg out of at the markets. He evidently took the horse through the hallway so that it could graze in the garden. My aunt said on one occasion, the house started to shake as if there was an earthquake only to find out that the horse's rear end was stuck in between the walls of the hallway and was kicking out panicking as my dad tried to take it through to the garden .

I didn't really know what I wanted to do when I left school. The Career's Officer would came to the school and interview every pupil on a one-to-one basis with the various job opportunities being extremely limited and if you told him (it was always a 'him'), that you wanted to be a 'Page 3 Sun photographer (not that the Sun was around at the time) or a professional footballer, he'd just laugh at you. The two choices that you had basically was to work with your hands in a factory or take on an apprenticeship or sit behind a desk in an office, me deciding on the latter.

So in 1959 I got a job at UDT (United Dominions Trust), at the time one of the biggest Hire Purchase/Loan companies in the world. The Head office was in Eastcheap in the city of London, with another large office in Cockfosters at the end of the Piccadilly underground line and two what they called 'collection offices,' one of which I worked in in Tottenham, backing onto Tottenham Marshes and being next door to Amstraad, Alan Sugar's first premises and the other in Edmonton, where Mike Smith the keyboard player of The Dave Clarke Five worked.

For lunch we'd very often go to the then Park Hotel by Northumberland Park Station, which is now a Spurs Merchandise Shop. We used to play snooker in there on their beautifully kept tables but one day, some guy came in and told everybody that Jimmy Greaves had been killed in a car crash, the place was distraught with grown men crying their eyes out. Fortunately, it was only a rumour obviously but it wasn't a very good experience at the time.

Leaving school at 15, I wasn't what you would describe as being 'academic' but somehow I got through the interview at 'UDT' probably albeit through my love of football and being able to play it quite well, although the person carrying out the interview not knowing that, as UDT were really into their football and had a team in the what was called London Banks League. The league was mainly made up of proper banks e.g. Lloyds, National Westminster, The Bank of England, Barclays and Coutts the Queens bank.

As I said in the 'Warm Up,' most companies/firms had their own football teams and pitches/facilities in those days but the London Banks League was something else. Many of the banks had their grounds in Beckenham, Lloyds being one of them who had underfloor heating in the dressing room and this being back in the 60s. Also the Bank of England's ground was a great place to play, they having a ten pin bowling alley in the basement of theirs which I suppose was one of the reasons why the England international team chose to train there at the time. Most of our away games were some distance from Tottenham where we were based but it wasn't a problem, as long as I got back on a Saturday evening so that I could go to my regular dancing and drinking venue which was The White Hart in Devonshire Lane.

Being only a 'Hire Purchase' company, I never did find out how U.D.T. were invited to play in the Banks League but so again were the London Polytechnic, the only other team to be in it not being a bank.

I don't think it helped that we (U.D.T.) not being a bank, were quite successful in winning the league and cup on a number of occasions. I remember one season, because of our success in the league and the cup, we got involved in a fixture pile up and we had to play London Polytechnic (Polly as they were called) at their ground late in the season on a Wednesday evening. We set off as we did for away games, in our 'Grey-Green' coach at about 4 p.m. having been let off early from work to travel round the North Circular Road, a.k.a. the A406 where their ground was situated in West London.

The North Circular then in the 60s, was the equivalent to what is now the M25 and as time got nearer and nearer to the rush hour so the traffic got denser. We were crawling along and our manager started to panic, thinking we wouldn't arrive at our opponents ground on time for kick off. This was obviously pre-mobile phone times but he noticed a telephone box up ahead, so he decided he would run to it and phone our opponents to let them know we were on our way. Just as our coach 'crawled' up to the phone box, one of the players put his head round the coach door and shouted to our manager "And tell 'Polly' to put the kettle on."

As I said, I was only fifteen when I joined U.D.T. and because of Spurs successful period at the time, I chose not to play on Saturday afternoons, which was when we played games, as I wanted to watch my beloved Spurs team, travelling around the country as I did to almost every game during the Double Winning season of 60-61. Us Spurs fans now are somewhat jealous of how City, United & Chelsea can throw money around to buy success but back in the 60s, it was us and Everton that were known as the rich boys of football.

I remember our first defeat of the 'double' season was in November, against Sheffield Wednesday 2-1 up at Hillsborough. It was a real murky November afternoon with the 'slag heaps' behind one end of the ground making the place even more depressing. Coincidentally, I'd met a girl during the summer of that year in a holiday camp on the Isle of Wight and never did get her address but she came from Parsons Cross, a district in Sheffield and as I was walking to the game I saw a bus with Parsons Cross on the front of it but the game was foremost on my mind.

I remember some of Sheffield Wednesday's team as if it was only yesterday, Springett in goal, Hills, Megson, Swan, Kaye, McAnerney, Johnny Fantham & Bronco Layne at centre forward, there's no doubt they were a formidable team albeit with Swan Kaye & Layne getting allegedly involved in some financial skulduggery that they got duly banned for. We came back to London on the train alighting at Finsbury Park Station, with the number of carriages being longer than the platform, so we had to get out of our carriage and walk along the track to the station, something you'd never be allowed to do now. I was so depressed, I remember saying to myself "I'm never going to watch Spurs play again" so disappointed that I was to see my mighty Spurs lose, I thought they were unbeatable. Of course, by the end of the week I was back at White hart Lane the next Saturday watching the team take our defeat out on Birmingham City 6-0.

Of course supporting the club through that season was a wonderful experience, culminating in us winning the cup at the end of it.

I remember before the kick off of the final, Princess Margaret was presented to the teams on the pitch and she showed her observance when she said to our captain Danny Blanchflower "Why have the Leicester City players got their surnames on the back of their track suits and you haven't on yours?" To which Danny said "Oh well ma'am, that's because we know all our players."

The other thing was, having had the opportunity of going to many away games, I kept many of the programmes relating to the games that I went to and collecting many more from various sources so much so I had almost a thousand of going back to pre-war games. It was only when, because of them just sitting in the loft and me having a daughter rather than a son, who isn't interested in football, I decided to sell them at auction held at Leicester's rugby union ground a few years ago where I got around the same amount of pounds for them that I had programmes.

Having witnessed Spurs success of winning the double, I thought there wasn't much else they could achieve in the future seasons apart from perhaps winning the '61-2 European Cup as it was then known, that we qualified for having won the previous season's 1st Division. We could have won it if we hadn't had been dumped out of the competition quite corruptitiously, if that's a proper word, by some odd decisions when we played Benfica in the two-legged semi-finals when we had a couple of goals disallowed for reasons only known to the referee. That said, the road to the semi-final started off with a bit of a scare. It was the first time Tottenham Hotspur had played in a European competition, albeit I think most fans thought that we were going to do quite well in it after the way we superbly played having won the League

& Cup Double. The games were played on a two-legged basis and we were drawn against a relatively unknown Polish team by the name of Gornik Zarbze, having to play the 1st leg away. It was a real wintery Wednesday afternoon and 'unbelievably' the result came over the radio that we had lost 4-2, the fans couldn't believe it they were in shock, perhaps we'd underestimated the other foreign teams in the competition. The 2nd leg at home was an all-ticket affair, with the fans having to queue up on a Sunday morning to get them, with the game being the 1st that I can ever remember whereby fans acquired their tickets in this manner. The ground held about 62,000 at the time, coincidentally about the same capacity as the new 'Tottenham Hotspur Stadium' with some fans starting to queue on the Saturday night. My dear old dad at the time, was working nights for London Transport at Tramway Avenue Bus Garage in Edmonton as a bus cleaner, most of them being the old trolleybuses that operated via a couple of poles extending from the roof of the bus to two electric parallel cables that ran high up above the roads suspended by poles spaced out on the kerbsides.

Now, here's a question for those that remember trolleybuses. As they were travelling along with the poles attached to the parallel cables above them, how did they go round a 90 degree corner at a road junction?

Well, as the bus approached the corner of the junction, the conductor would jump off the bus holding his, over the shoulder leather satchel that contained the money that he'd collected so that it wouldn't fall out and ran in front of the bus to a pole that would have a metal chain with a 'loop' at the end of it. As the bus approached the pole, the conductor would pull down hard on the chain so that in effect, similar to points on a railway line, the poles on top of the bus would switch over to the overhead suspended cables for the new road that the bus would be travelling on, the conductor would then release the chain for the points to go back to their original positions and then the conductor would run round the corner to jump back on the bus to continue it's journey. Many think, that the conductor re-positioned the poles with a very long bamboo pole that was kept under the chassis of the bus but that was a myth, that was only used if a pole on the bus came of the overhead suspended cables.

Because my dad's shift would finish around 5/6 o'clock in the morning, he would go straight to the ground and get in the queue and I would go and relieve him about 7.30 so that he could go home and catch up on his sleep with the tickets going on sale at 9. By the time the tickets went on sale, the queue would go from the main entrance in the High Road round to Paxton Road behind one of the goals, along Worcester Avenue, which was behind the stand that was opposite to the main West Stand then along Park Lane to Northumberland Park Station then 'up' Northumberland Park itself, it seemed to go on for miles and miles but in an orderly fashion, I never saw any queue jumping or anything.

I think all the Spurs fans were in trepidation as to how the 2nd leg would go but all to no avail, as we were soon 3-0 up early on in the 2nd leg which wiped out the two goal deficit that we were in after the 1st leg. We went on to win quite easily 8-1 but Gornik scored the best goal of the game, a thunderous volley by a guy named Ernest Pohl, in fact it was one of the most memorable goals I've ever witnessed at White Hart Lane to this day. The weird thing was, we had at left back in our team who played in the games, Ron Henry, whose hobby was to breed budgerigars in his home in Ponders End, Enfield. When Ron retired, he later became trainer/physio for the Spurs youth team and he told me once when I was having a cup of tea in his presence at Spurs training ground in Chigwell, that by coincidence, because of his love of ornithology he went on a 'bird-watching trip' to the Scilly Isles only to meet once again the aforementioned Ernest Pohl there, as he had a similar hobby and love of birds. I don't know if

Ernest was living in Poland at the time and travelled all the way there but it was a hell of a coincidence.

I thought it time to return to playing, so I decided to turn out for my employers U.D.T., albeit I had to make my debut in their reserve side rather than the 1st team. I remember my debut being my initiation test, as the team was pinned up on the company's notice board on the Friday previous to the game on Saturday, with my name on it. I noticed that the left half of our team had the name 'Riddle.' Whilst we were getting changed prior to kick off on the Saturday, I asked our captain what the chap Riddle's christian name was to which he replied "Jimmy" which it wasn't, he was just winding me up with the cockney jargon slang in mind. I didn't realise it at the time and called the fella 'Jimmy' throughout the game, not receiving a single pass from him or having any communication whatsoever throughout the 90 minutes. It was a shame really, because I really took to the guy, he had such a sweet left foot. Why is it that left footed players look so comfortable on the ball, the likes of Jim Baxter, Ferenc Puscas, Lionel Messi, our own Mousa Dembele and I have to say reluctantly Arsenal's Liam Brady. It seems to me, right footed and right handed sportsman don't understand what left footed and left handed sportsman are going to do with a ball, they're so difficult to play against, they see the game with a completely different angled view, it's all to do with the brain. That said, I write left handed and I used to get the cane in school just because to be left-handed was considered to be something to do with 'the devil' and wasn't acceptable.

I was 15 at the time and I was also invited to play in a Walthamstow U-16 league team run by a great fella by the name of Bill Bedford. Bill lived in Bennetts Close, blocks of flats at the top of Northumberland Park where it meets Tottenham High Road. He was a quintessential Sunday morning type of manager, not knowing a great deal about the tactical side of the game. I remember in a 'training session' we once had when Bill was trying to drill us into playing 'give it and go football.' Some of the lads couldn't take on board this 'give it and go football' stuff and at one time he got so frustrated he shouted at one of the lads "You're going before you're giving it." Hilarious. He also once told one of our players to 'man-mark' a player of the opposition and "Not to leave his side." Our player complied with Bill's instruction all game and even went over and stood next to him at half-time while the player was sucking his orange while his manager was giving his team the half-time team talk. He really looked after us lads as a real father figure. He'd invite as many of the lads who wanted to go round his flat on a Saturday night with his family just to socialise before the game the next day, many of us accepting his invitation just because he had a very attractive daughter Penny. Somehow, we entered the league under the name of 'Queens,' which I hastened to add we weren't but it was a very competitive league with another team called 'Angel' in it. Angels they weren't either, they were as 'hard as nails' their centre half being the hard man David Webb who went on to play for Chelsea extremely successfully.

That said, they were a very good side with some very technically gifted players winning the league during the two seasons that we were in it. I remember though in one game, we had the audacity to take the lead against them just before half-time. When they came out in the second half talk about 'wounded animals,' they really came at us both physically and with an intensity. With a few minutes only gone, they were awarded a free kick just outside our penalty area. Their player who took it, rifled the ball into the top corner with our keeper, who we called endearingly 'Clanger' because he was prone to a mistake, flapping at fresh air. A few minutes later they attacked us again with one of their players hitting a shot from again just outside the box that again was aiming for the top corner but this time, our 'Clanger' got to it and tipped it over the bar for a corner.

As I walked into the six yard box to wait for the corner to be taken, I said to 'Clanger,' "Great save mate" to which he replied, "To be honest Johnny. I was still diving to try to stop the shot from the free kick that they scored from."

According to my birth certificate I was christened JOHN RAY but when I was very young, I adopted the name of JOHNNY RAY, I think in part due to the American born pop singer of the 50s who was partially deaf with a question mark about his sexuality albeit with his christian name being spelt Johnnie rather than Johnny as I spelt mine.

He was very popular in the UK mainly with the females having hit records such as 'Walking In The Rain' & 'Not Tonight Josephine' in fact, I remember when in the early 50s, my mum took me to the London Palladium just in the hope that she might see him arrive at the same time telling as many of the other girls and ladies that were there that my name was Johnny Ray, pointing at me at the same time.

I suppose I would have been embarrassed if I'd known what the word meant, which I didn't at 10 years of age.

I liked being referred to as Johnny, as I thought it very endearing but as I got older I preferred to be known as John, as I always thought that 'Johnny' was ok if you were a car dealer or something similar but it didn't seem conducive in the line of work that I found myself in as I got older, that said, I'm again often referred to as 'Johnny' up here in Norfolk where I now live especially as I'm in the autumn years of my life, which I like as it makes me feel younger again.

During one game in the Walthamstow League, many of which were played on Hackney Marshes, the referee decided he had reason to book me, rather for something I said I should imagine, as I couldn't tackle to save my life. He called me over and said "Name?" I replied 'Johnny Ray' so he, thinking I was taking the piss referring to the pop singer replied "Yeah? And I'm Sir Winston Churchill get off." My colleagues thought it horrendous until they realised they would only have ten players, so by them convincing the ref it was my name really I was invited back onto the pitch to continue to participate. Coincidentally around the same time, a good friend of mine Micky Eason, the brother of Les Eason, he of Barnet, Enfield Town & Finchley back in the 60s, Les being regarded as the equivalent of Jimmy Greaves of the England amateur side at the time, got booked giving his name as Mickey Mouse. He got sent off and his club fined for not having a 'Mickey Mouse' registered on their books.

Our home pitch was on the infamous Hackney Marshes, I say 'home' pitch,' as we'd be playing on any of the 104 pitches allocated to us at home one week and on another away the next. There were so many goalposts, albeit without nets, the front of the posts were painted white with the back of them painted green to eliminate any confusion so that you didn't shoot in the wrong goal if you were on another pitch. To get to Hackney Marshes from 'North' Tottenham, we would jump on a 149 bus to Stamford Hill and get off by the salt beef bar opposite the old Stamford Hill Odeon. We'd then go round the corner to catch a bus to Clapton Pond and then a single decker bus to Hackney Marshes. Every time we made the journey, we'd pass Homerton Hospital where a wall would have a plaque on it saying 'Bill Stickers Will Be Prosecuted.' Every time we went past it someone would say "I see they haven't caught Bill Stickers yet." When we reached the age of 16 with the Walthamstow League being of an U-16 age group, we had to disband the team but Bill Bedford our manager, moved down to Cheshunt in Hertfordshire to live on an estate that Russ Ballard, the guitarist of the group Unit 4 + 2 led by the singer Buster Meakle they of the record 'Concrete and Clay' lived on. Cliff Richard also lived there at the time, incidentally my cousin played drums in the Drifters, Cliff's early days backing group before he formed The Shadows to back him. Moving into the area it came to Bill Bedford's attention that there was a local Sunday league, The Waltham & Forest District League in operation, so Bill got as many of us together as he could again, plus some better players and entered a team into the league originally calling us The Coach & Horses, a pub he used to frequent in Waltham Cross who used to sponsor us, changing the name eventually to Cheshunt United. I have to say, we were young still all around the 17 years of age mark but a good team, we had players that could easily have been comfortable in a higher grade of football not least professionally, players like Tony Millbanks and Johnny Knott. We were like the Busby Babes of the league. We went from the lowest Division 3 to Division 1 in two seasons, the second season getting to the league's cup semi-finals doing a real giant killing act on the way knocking out some of the teams in the Premier Division. Mike England, the one-time Spurs & Wales centre-half came to see us play once at Grundy Park in Cheshunt, which was our home ground. I say 'came to' see us, I think really he was just walking his dog and stopped to have a look.

We got drawn against Brimsdown in the semi-final who were one of the two top teams at the time in the Premier Division. There was a period of about five weeks between the quarter finals and the semis which created a period of excitement, apprehension and a certain amount of nervousness.

So our big day came. We arrived at the venue and couldn't believe the number of people that had come to see what all the fuss was about with us being of such a relatively young age, some hoping that we would make another giant killing. We entered the field of play with not a sight of daylight between the crowd around the perimeter of the pitch. We won the toss and gave Brismsdown the opportunity of kicking off but as the referee put his whistle to his mouth, we witnessed Bill Bedford running onto she pitch screaming at the ref "Wait, we haven't named our sub," which you only had one of at the time but you wouldn't be able to bring him on if he wasn't named before the kick off. Micky Eason our captain, he of 'Mickey Mouse' fame shouted at Bill "It's ok I've dealt with it" so Bill, embarrassed by all this turned on his heels to run off the pitch which was very muddy, only to slip and fall on his face, all in his best suit which he wore for the game that got covered in mud.

Well if that wasn't enough embarrassment, Brimsdown kicked off, their centre-forward passing to their inside forward who in turn passed the ball back to their centre half who took one touch of it forward and 'hoofed' it into the sky towards our goal. The ball took one bounce right on the edge of our penalty area. Our keeper Sydie Nash, whether it was nerves or not, took one step forward one step back, again one step forward with the ball sailing over his head into the goal. All this and we'd only been on the pitch for two minutes. The crowd thought it all hilarious but it was so embarrassing for us. We went on to lose the game 4-1 with our reputation in tatters.

Actually I went to visit Bill in the Roman Urn pub in Cheshunt many years later as I'd heard he'd had a heart attack and I wanted to see how he was. He hadn't changed his habits, he was still drinking heavily and smoking as he used to. I said to him "Bill, are you doing the right thing by smoking?" He replied, having fought in the 2nd World War "If those fucking Japs couldn't kill me these little bastards won't" pointing to his lit up cigarette, typical Bill.

So, reverting back to working for and playing for U.D.T. I was promoted to the 1st team at the age of 16 playing in the London Banks League with the majority of facilities of the clubs being superb. As I've said previously with Lloyds having underfloor heating in the dressing rooms and The Bank of England a ten pin bowling alley in their basement, ours weren't so salubrious being situated at Ashton Playing Fields in Woodford. Many of you will know of it, it can be seen if you look down, on the left of the M11 travelling south where it meets the A406 North Circular Road where all those annoying speed cameras are.

The standard and level of play and players was pretty good as well, the banks having the luxury of selecting players from almost all of their branches throughout London, that's why our success in winning the league on more than one occasion and cup was such an achievement, as we only had the two collection offices, as said previously, Tottenham and Edmonton to pick from. That said, we could have been better than we were if we could have convinced Mike Smith in our Edmonton office to play instead of him pursuing his dream of making it big time in the music scene, which as we all know he did as the good-looking keyboard player for The Dave Clarke Five. The reason I'm saying this, is that Mike was actually in the youth set up as a centre half for Tottenham during the period they won the 60-61 double.

Whilst I was working and playing for U.D.T., I was introduced by a working colleague of mine to a guy by the name of Tony Goodwin who, as it turned out, I became really friendly with and not a bad footballer himself. Apart from socialising with him in pubs and clubs, we also went to watch Spurs together if either of us weren't playing when they were. One day back in the 60s, we went to Upton Park to watch us play West Ham. Tony lived in Ponders End so he got the 149 bus in Hertford Road up to Tottenham where I was waiting for him at Park Lane. When I saw him hanging out of the on/off platform of the bus at the rear of it, I jumped on to join him to continue on to South Tottenham station to catch the train to Barking where we had to change for Upton Park.

When we got off the bus at South Tottenham, we were walking along to the station to catch the 1 o'clock train when we saw a train going across the bridge of the High Road. We and others that were on the bus, all going to the game panicked and started running thinking we were going to miss it. As we ran into the station, even the ticket guy was caught out and shouted at all of us to "pay at the other end." We ran up the stairs only to find that the train was a 'goods' train that trundled through the station without stopping with the train that we needed to catch coming in a few minutes later. We got to Barking and changed onto the underground to get to Upton Park albeit we didn't have any tickets. So Tony and I had a discussion and decided that instead of telling the ticket collector that we came from South Tottenham, we said that we'd come from Barking instead to save us money. When we arrived and went up the stairs to where the ticket machines were, we told a guy being an 'Underground personnel' about our predicament. He responded by saying "I don't take money but those two gentlemen will" pointing at two British Railway policemen. So we told them the same story, only for them to split Tony and I up, with the one that I was with asking me what my name was and where I lived in Barking, given that was where we told them we'd come from. I just clawed a name out of the air albeit using a name of a lad that I'd been at school with, I replied "John Aldridge and I live at No. 9 Baker Road, Barking." The copper shouted to Tony "Oi, what's his name and where does he live.? Of course Tony didn't have a clue what I'd told the copper. We got nicked and fined quire heavily I recall and I suppose somewhere in the ether I have a criminal record.

We got to Upton Park and as you did in those days, we paid our money and stood where we wanted, mixing with the oppositions supporters as you did then. West Ham had quite a few black lads in their team at the time, unlike Spurs who didn't. Their team was read out over the tannoy, names like John Charles, Clyde Best & Ade Cocker who were all black lads, which prompted a guy behind us, who I assume was a Spurs supporter to shout out "Fuck me, are this lot doing a season at the New Victoria?"

Which was the venue for the Black & White Minstrel Show in London that was extremely popular at the time. It didn't end there, just after, the police moved into the crowd behind the goal to take out a black fella who had a Hammers scarf on and proceeded to 'frog-march' the lad along the running track of the pitch. As they passed us, the same guy who made the previous comment shouted "Fuck me, they've only arrested their substitute as well." I told these stories to a West Ham fan who owns a book shop in Cromer up here in Norfolk where I now live. He said, when he used to go to Upton Park and around the same time , he experienced a similar situation whereby during a game, standing a little way back from the pitch surrounding wall, Harry Redknapp, when he was then a frail looking lad in his teens and playing for The Hammers, was 'bombing' down the wing only to be barged into said surrounding wall by some burly left back of the opposition. He said, Harry went down with an almighty bang and stayed down for some time, to be attended to by the St. John's Ambulance Brigade. He went on to say, that a guy brushed passed him from behind where he was standing, ran down to the wall and leant over it shouting "Stay there Harry we're fetching your mum."

The same guy also told me, that whilst watching a game at West Ham, The Hammers went 1-0 down early on with one of the fellas in the crowd he was with saying "I know I should have gone down the Arsenal" as they were playing at home the same day. About ten minutes later the opposition scored again, with the same fella saying "See, I knew I should have gone down the Arsenal." All the lads around him got hold of him and threw him over the perimeter wall onto the surrounding track of the pitch. The police came running over thinking the guy was going to run onto the pitch but the police were convinced of his story of what happened and they attempted to throw him back into the crowd but every time and everywhere they did along the terracing, the crowd closed ranks shouting to the police "Take him down The Arsenal."

I have to say, racism didn't seem to be an issue at the time, that's why you could get away with putting on shows like The Black & White Minstrel Show as mentioned in the paragraph before last, not like it is now with the awareness of it and general political correctness being brought to people's attention. When I lived in Tottenham throughout the 50s, 60s & 70s, excuse me from being naïve but I don't recall there being any racism, I and my family definitely weren't, our neighbours were black and we got on very well, we all seemed to live in harmony you had to. In the 50s. Guy Gibson, the leader of the factual Dambusters had a dog he named Nigger, the same name coincidentally that my mum and dad gave our black cat, maybe in innocence maybe in ignorance but we didn't have a cat flap and my dad used to go out in the street to get him in at around 10 at night shouting "Nigger! Nigger!" No-one seemed to take offence. Of course there were 'racist' jokes about ethnic groups as there were about Irish people but there was no real hatred in telling them. It's like the sitcoms of the day, Till Death Us Do Part & Love Thy Neighbour, they were hilarious and no-one seemed to take offence, especially black people that I knew who found them hilarious to. That said, the only story that I did find racially offensive and to show how fickle football fans are was when I and some friends travelled down to Southampton to their old 'The Dell' ground to see Spurs play a Wednesday night midweek game. Incidentally, whenever we went to away games I always tried to fit-in local areas of interest e.g before we went Southampton, I took us all to Hamble, a village along the coast where they filmed the TV programme Howards Way and I did a similar thing when we went up to Manchester to see us play City. One of my friends had to drop off a photocopier as a salesman for a company to a client in Yorkshire, so I took us all to Holmfirth where they filmed Last Of The Summer Wine and had lunch in the café that was used in the filming in the village before we'd set off across The Pennines into Lancashire, it was great fun. In the City game, I remember our centre half at the time Richard Gough, getting a right old ticking off by the referee for a late tackle he made. The reprimand seemed to go on for ages, which made a City fan near us shout "Hurry up ref, we've got to go to work in the morning" which made a Spurs fan reply, "Well some of you have," referring to the lack of work up in the north at the time in comparison to down south.

Southampton at the time, had some good players such as, Shilton in goal, Dave Watson at centre-half and Keegan and Mike Channon up front. We were in a somewhat transitional phase having won the FA Cup in 1981&82 with a few of the players either getting on a bit or suffering from long term injuries, Garth Crooks being one of them. I remember an incident when we got a corner and it was taken reaching the far post. Shilton went up for it but somehow lost the flight of the ball and only succeeded in palming it down to Garth who was standing on the corner of the six yard box. Now Garth, who had been out of the side with a serious knee problem, had just got back in the team and seemed all game to have a problem in getting his confidence back. The ball took one' high' bounce in front of him, he just couldn't decide by what part of his anatomy he should control it, his foot, thigh, knee, chest but a fan standing behind us tried to make up his mind for him by shouting "Head it wog!" As said, that just goes to show how fickle and ignorant fans are, when Garth was playing in the '81 final when he scored in the replay, the same fella was probably calling him 'Garthie Baby' or 'Crooksy' in an endearing way, much loved as he was as a Spurs player.

I told this story once to Richard Digance the comedian, when he was performing at the Royal Standard pub in Walthamstow close to Blackhorse Road, underground station. He'd been on stage singing and telling his stories. one of them being that he grew up as a West Ham fan and lived with his parents on the 8th floor of a block of flats right behind one of West Ham's goals but he said they had to move, because every time they got a penalty, Ray Stewart their Scottish right back would take it and break one of his mum and dad's (8th floor) windows. I was able to talk with him during the interval as my friends and I were standing in a corner of the bar where he came round to get a drink. I was getting a round in and as I turned to pass some drinks over my shoulder standing right behind me was Richard himself. He sort of apologised for being in the way saying, "Sorry, it's crowded in here isn't it?" Well I said, It's your fault for being here." I told him I liked his story about Ray Stewart, then we continued to swap anecdotes, one of mine being the Garth Crooks one which I have to say he really laughed at.

I saw him again doing a one man show at Cromer Pier when I moved up to Norfolk in the 90s, the first thing he said when he came on stage was " This is the nearest I've been to Russia." Mind you, that wasn't as funny as what the warm up and supporting comedian said that was on with him. He was a black guy, about 6ft. 5ins. tall dressed in an orange suit and black roll neck jumper. He came on stage and the first thing he said was "What a place this is to get to." Now I don't know if you know Cromer but the town itself is high up above where the pier is situated, with ramps leading down to it for vehicle access to the pier in rather obscure places. The guy went onto say, remembering that the show started at 7.30 " I got here at 4 o'clock and I was driving around for what seemed ages up there (pointing to the town) trying to find out how I could get down to the pier. In the end I got so fed up so I shouted to what seemed like a local fella, " Oi John, how d'ya get down to the pier?" He replied "How did you know my name was John?" To which I replied "I guessed." To which he replied "Well guess how to get down to the fucking pier then."

The thing about racism is, it doesn't relate to just black & white people. If you remember the story I told earlier about me as a lad and my friends playing cricket in Baronet Road where I lived near the Spurs ground, I mentioned in it a street lamp that we used to use as a wicket. Well there was a Jamaican family who lived just a couple of houses up from it and they very often came out to play with us, the father, uncle and their sons and being Jamaicans they were all very formidable cricketers. At the other end of Baronet Road where it met St. Pauls Road, lived another black family and I remember saying to the Jamaican family "Why don't you go and knock your friends up from down the road and get them to play?" But they refused, as in their words they were Jamaicans and the other family were Africans and they didn't see eye to eye.

On the subject of 'ethnicity.' Given the high percentage of ethnic groups living within Tottenham and the surrounding areas, you don't see many black or Asian faces in the 62k crowd of a game at The Tottenham Stadium when Spurs are playing at home these days. I don't know whether it's because the ethnic population don't have the history of the club in their hearts, given that many of them have only moved into the area in relatively later years, or whether quite simply they can't afford it. When I do go down there for a home game walking to the ground or The Antwerp Arms before kick off, I often go past barber shops and see the local black guys either having their hair cut or just standing or sitting in there 'chilling.' I often feel like saying, "Hey man, don't you know your local team is playing just down the road, why aren't you in there supporting them?" Mind you, I expect things will change as time moves on as more local ethnic lads are actually born in the area and will relate more to the club and they take up the season tickets that the indigenous white people who have retained their season tickets having moved out of the area where they were brought up either give them up or 'pop their socks', again, if they can afford it that is.

I had a cousin Tony Hemmings, who was a really good sportsman. He was a good centre-forward and he also played for Middlesex second elevens at cricket. He lived in Edmonton and went to Edmonton County School, as did his brother, my cousin Alby and some to be famous people like Bruce Forsyth, Johnny Haynes the Fulham footballer, Larry Lamb the actor and Tony Marchi who played for Spurs in the 50s/60s. My cousin Alby, Tony's brother, was a very good friend of Bruce Forsythe who then lived in Victoria Road, Edmonton around the corner to where Alby and Tony lived. Bruce himself was a big Spurs fan, albeit he has admitted that he would go to see Spurs one week when they were at home and the Arsenal the next week when they were at home with his dad. Similarly, I remember, although me and my dad were massive Spurs fans, once going to Highbury on a Boxing day in the 50s just because we wanted something to do as Spurs were away. We caught I think it was the No.279 trolley bus to go from Tottenham High Road to Finsbury Park to walk to Highbury. There must have been almost 70 thousand people there that day, me and my dad hanging on to the railings high up at the rear of the North Stand. I do remember Billy Wright playing for Wolves that day though.

It reminds me of an 80s TV series 'Shine On Harvey Moon,' starring Kenneth Cranham. It was about a soldier who'd come back from the 2nd World War to be with his family. His son was playing for his school team on a Saturday morning and 'Harvey' said to his son, "If you play well, I'll take you to Highbury this afternoon to see Arsenal play." The son did, so off they went to Highbury with the son having his boots tied round his neck by the laces as kids did in the day. When they arrived, there was no-one to be seen apart from a commissionaire on the main gate. Harvey said to him, "I thought the first team were at home today" to which the commissionaire replied, "They are but at the moment they're playing all their home games at Tottenham's White Hart Lane" as Highbury was being used as literally an arsenal for weapons. Harvey's son said to his dad all excitedly "Can we get the bus down there dad?" To which Harvey replied

"You're kidding, I'm not going to see Arsenal play a home game at White Hart Lane." That's like a guy in my village where I now live in Norfolk, he's a massive Spurs fan albeit coincidentally he was born in Islington. He reckoned he hates Arsenal so much he won't eat bacon because it's 'red & white.'

That reminds me, why don't 'they' ever show repeats of the old black and white 'football' related films anymore like, 'The Arsenal Stadium Mystery,' 'On The Beat,' where Norman Wisdom plays a policeman and referees lads playing football in the street blowing his whistle to make a decision only to be converged on by many other 'beat' policeman having heard the trill of his whistle and Arthur Askey's 'The Love Match,' where he plays a train driver driving the train at speed because he's late for a game he wanted to go to?

My dad hated the Arsenal. He took myself and my cousin Ian up to London to see the Changing Of The Guard one Sunday. We went from Wood Green on the Piccadilly tube line where we had to pass through the Arsenal Station. As the doors opened, he instructed me and my cousin to "Hold our noses," which we did until the doors closed and the train left the station. The other passengers must have thought we were mad, especially me and my cousin being 28, no we weren't really were just young boys. Good fun though. Mind you, I heard Talksport's Paul Hawkesbee telling a similar story recently whereby he said he 'boos' when he goes through Gillespie Road, the former name of 'Arsenal' station, he refuses to call and relate to the Piccadilly Line station as 'Arsenal.' That's the thing with 'The Arsenal,' they don't seem to have any self identity. 'Arsenal' isn't a place, they're like Port Vale or Queen of the South they don't exist and represent a true area. A 'Gooner' friend told me that 'they' only came over to North London from the south because of the underground network, as they thought they'd get bigger crowds as there was no underground stations in and around Woolwich at the time.

As said, my dad was a big fan of Spurs albeit in his later years, although we only lived about a half a mile from the ground, his interest did taper off somewhat, especially when they weren't being successful. I remember saying to him once on the day of a home game, "Aren't you going to the game this afternoon?" To which he replied "No, they don't come and see me when I'm not very good."

Going back to my cousin Tony, he's sporting opportunities sadly came to an end, when in his early twenties, he lost his sight when as a postman and collecting sacks of mail, he was blinded by a robber who sprayed something into his eyes in an attack on a post office in Park Lane, the thoroughfare that lay behind the south end of the Spurs ground.

He unfortunately never recovered his sight but he never lost his personality and sense of humour. He was a great and funny guy living to a comparatively old age with his Golden Labrador that he was allocated after his accident being by his side for many of his years. I remember, he and his wife came round to my mum and dad's, who lived in a warden controlled flat in Tramway Avenue, Edmonton for tea one Sunday evening. There were six of us and we were sitting round the table chatting. Now Tony always spoke in a way as though he'd actually seen things, ignoring his blindness. He said to me "Did you 'SEE' Spurs play last Wednesday John, didn't they play well?" Because he spoke in the way he did, subconsciously I just nodded until my dad had a go at me and said "Don't nod at him he can't see you." The Sunday although sunny, had been a really cold and frosty one. Tony said to me he had been over Pymmes Park in the morning to 'watch' the football, a park in Edmonton where a number of games would be played that were in the Edmonton Sunday League, the league not being affiliated to the F.A. I said to him, "How did you get around the park without walking onto the pitches?" He replying that his dog knew where to go and avoid the pitches and anyway, with the white stick that he had he could feel where the concreted paths were. He went onto say, he'd 'seen' a great game between a red team and a yellow team that quizzically made me ask "Now wait a minute Tony, how do you know the reds were playing the yellows?" To which he replied, "Because you can hear the crowd shouting 'Come on you reds or come on you yellows.' It was amazing and made me feel so humble, it was as if he was hearing life through a radio. He loved a drink with his friends down the pub, as did I and during a conversation that we had about pubs he threw in the observation that you'd only hear Jamaican/African voices in a pub never Asian, an observation that never came to my mind me being able to see.

Another thing just to prove that racism wasn't so much an issue at the time, well most certainly between me and my 'white' friends during the 60s.70s, was that we all used to stand on what was known as the 'shelf' on the first tier of the old East Stand at White Hart Lane and there was always a black guy who we didn't really know who stood with us, we called him 'Chalky' and he'd cheer the Spurs team on by shouting "Come on you whites" grinning at us after every time he shouted it.

We thought him hilarious and we loved him and he us.

From the shelf that I mentioned, I've witnessed some great games at Tottenham, the 13-2 victory in the F.A. Cup over Crewe Alexandria in 1959, the 2-1 victory over Sheffield Wednesday in 1961 which in effect gave us the double and the 2-1 victory over Benfica in 1962, albeit we did go out on goal difference, I'll say again, unfairly.

In the early days when I stood on the shelf around the 14/15 years of age mark, we used to have a challenge of getting into the seats high up above it in the East Stand. We could never afford seats, so me and a friend used to leave the shelf about 20 minutes from the end as they used to open the gates of the seating stand to let people out if they wanted to leave early. There was always a guy on the gate stopping people from coming in late into the game but we used to hang around and when he wasn't looking we'd rush in up the stairs and hide until we could sit in a seat that an early leaver would vacate. The guy on the gate would never catch us, we were much too quick for him. The thing is though, I remember we were watching us play the Busby Babes of Manchester United in 1958, the season before their horrific plane crash, Duncan Edwards, Roger Byrne, Tommy Taylor et al and we did 'the seat challenge' during it. Spurs were winning 2-0 and playing really well, I remember Johnny Brooks scoring one of the goals. We left the shelf to go downstairs to the gate to get up into the seats but by the time we'd left the shelf and got up to the seated East Stand, United had scored two goals in the space of about 10 minutes and we drew the game. I never did see their goals, no Match Of The Day then.

Having been at U.D.T. for 4 years or so, I decided sitting behind a desk as I was chasing late loan payments wasn't for me anymore, I decided to move on but to do what? I didn't have a trade but whatever I decided to do I had to get a job with a company that would be sympathetic with me getting off work in midweek early, as at the time I'd signed for Barnet in the then Southern League for a very short period but a comparatively longer one with Leyton in the Athenian League. In the end I had two choices, one was to join some friends of mine, brothers by the name of Tony & Johnny at Charringtons the brewery in Brantwood Road, Tottenham. Their dad got me the opportunity to go there as he was a senior foreman but it would have meant me sweeping the yards until somebody was sick, or on holiday, so that I could go out on the lorries delivering beer until of course somebody left, so that I could permanently go out delivering. I remember the lads on the delivery lorries were earning ridiculous amounts of money, a lot of it possibly not quite kosher, as it was from barrels that they had left over on the lorries at the end of the day somehow, that they then sold onto publicans at a cheaper rate than what they would normally buy them for.

Tony & Johnny were very good footballers, they played for Highgate Redwing with Rod Stewart. They told me a story, amongst many others about Rod, whereby the team had got through to the quarter finals of a national competition that they'd entered. They used to train Tuesday & Thursday nights but on the Thursday night previous to the quarter final Rod didn't attend because Maggie May had gone to No. 1 in the charts and he had to be on Top Of The Pops to perform it. Highgate Redwing went on to win the game on the following Saturday without Rod, who had been left out of the team by his uncle who was managing the side, because he hadn't attended training. In fact, Highgate Redwing went on to win the competition but Rod didn't play in it again because his uncle refused to change a winning side.

They did tell me though, that after they won the quarter-final without Rod, he did watch the game and invited all the players and everyone associated with the club to a local pub afterwards saying that 'Drinks were on him.' After the drinks had been served, Rod started to feel his pockets saying that he didn't have any money on him he'd forgotten it, albeit he did the same thing in the semi-final that they won with everyone not surprisingly being a bit to say the least unbelieving, when he said again "Drinks are on me" only for him to open up an attaché case on the bar with bundles of money loosely falling out of it.

I did see Rod once and asked him about the accusations but he said as in the song, "I Don't Wanna Talk About It." Not really only joking.

That said, Rod did throw a massive party for them on the night of the final which they won, at his 'mansion' in Virginia Water having moved there from Broadwalk in Southgate.

Because the brothers Johnny & Tony were very connected with the publicans they delivered beer to, they always had their ears to the ground as to when entertainment was on, you know the 'blue' nights that were popular with the lads in the day and because of it, they always got the best tables by the dance floors where the strippers performed. I remember one night, we went to a pub called The Heathcote & Star in Leytonstone which was holding one of those nights with Mike Reid the comedian and one time actor of Eastenders comparing it. Now myself and a guy by the name of Brian Ellerbeck,'Eller' as he was known who some of you may remember as one of the guys who sold peanuts around the track of the White Hart Lane pitch in the 60s/70s/80s, throwing the bags of nuts into the crowd in the hope that he would get his money thrown back at him, attended a presentation night in aid of the Edmonton Sunday League at the Regal Rooms which were situated over the top of the Regal cinema in Edmonton which again, Mike Reid compared. Although The Regal was a cinema, in the 60 s it did 'double up' as a music venue and I remember seeing The Rolling Stones perform there around 1965, when they were on tour supporting Bo Diddley.The bizarre thing was, a lot of The Stones early 'stuff' was cover versions of the likes of Bo Diddley and Chuck Berry songs, like Diddley's 'Hey Mona' and Berry's 'Carol' and when they supported both the artists on tour The Stones would do their versions in their set, with Bo Diddley & Chuck Berry singing them again in theirs which was weird. The Regal Edmonton later became The Sundown, where I saw amongst others Roy Wood's Wizard and the marvellous Dr. John who promoted his gig by playing on the back of a 'low loader truck' along Edmonton Fore Street on the day before it, this was all before the building turned into a supermarket which is what it is now.

The Edmonton Sunday League whose presentation night I and 'Eller' attended, was of a very high standard, not least because it was the only league around that wasn't affiliated to the F.A. It was almost a 'pirate' league meaning that really good players that were contracted to good amateur sides e.g. local to us, Barnet, Finchley & Cheshunt could all play for teams in it. The team that was most successful throughout the league's reign was Park United, which at one time had the likes of Les Picking, Vic Lucas, Billy Ratty in it and Les Eason who I've said earlier was the England amateur team's Jimmy Greaves. I got invited to play for a team in the league by the name of Britannia. Ian Thomas (Thommo as he was known) their captain and incidentally the brother-in-law of, as some of you may remember Bobby Keech, the Fulham 60s centre-half , invited me, an invitation I took up for a few games until I couldn't handle it anymore. They were, for a want of a better word 'rough' side, comprising the likes of Dave Barnett, who played in goal for Spurs at some level at some time, Kenny Stapleton and a Greek lad by the name of Baz. They were a great bunch of blokes if you knew them or on their side but if you didn't or weren't, then God help you. They were the only team that I ever witnessed run OFF the pitch to go into the stands to attack the fans rather than the other way round, it happened at the Henry Barrass Stadium in Edmonton. Anyway I digress, back to Mike Reid and the Regal Rooms. He took umbrage to 'Eller' who, when getting up to 'take a leak' during his act said something to him to embarrass him in front of the audience, as comedians do in these situations. 'Eller' responded to Mike Reid by saying something to him through smiling teeth. Mike Reid responded by saying to Eller "You say something back to me again and I'll knock those smiling teeth down your fucking throat." Charming.

Now I don't know if Mike Reid was actually a Spurs fan but he did live in Argyle Road just off Tottenham High Road and spitting distance from the Spurs ground. He also went to Rowland Hill School, the school I've mentioned earlier in the book which Dickie Moss was the headmaster of. Actually, there was an ally in Argyle Road where Mike Reid lived that led to the High Road and opposite the alley was a sports shop by the name of Elsey's where most of the Spurs players bought their boots. The proprietor once told me, that John White the inside forward of the 'Double Side' couldn't stand the wool of socks touching his feet so 'Elsey's' used to stick cotton wool inside his boots and John White would then cut off the soles of his football socks.

Back to the Heathcote. The brothers Johnny & Tony acquired about twelve tickets for us one night and we were given a big oval table to sit round in the best position by the dance floor where the 'strippers' would carry out their act but because Eller and I had had the experience of witnessing how Mike Reid performed previously, when the show was about to start Eller and I hot footed it up the stairs from the bar where we were to sit at the table furthest away from the end where the dance floor was in the event another situation might occur with Mike Reid. I have to say, he didn't disappoint. After he did his comedy stint he said to the audience, all of them being lads "Right, the girls are coming on now to do their acts and I tell you now, there'll be no touching, if so, that will be the end of it and the girls won't continue to perform." A guy who was with us, an Irish lad by the name of Tony McGurck, a good footballer himself having been on Spurs books as a youth during the 'Double' season, chose to sit at the 'head of the table' saying he "didn't give a fuck about Mike Reid." A stripper came on and when she finished her act naked, she sat on Tony's lap. Now I don't know to this day whether Tony did touch her or not but she jumped up as if she had been which emanated in Mike Reid jumping off the stage towards Tony raging "I fucking warned you didn't I?" Well everybody to a man on our table, even Eller and I jumped up as one with the intention of defending Tony only for Mike Reid to turn on his heels to return to the stage saying to the rest of the audience laughingly "That frightened 'em didn't it? With the show fortunately carrying on.

I must say, I've always been very envious of stand up comedians and 'after dinner speakers,' I'd love to have been one myself as I loved telling jokes and anecdotes to friends but I never felt confident of standing up in front of people to tell them and retorting to the jibes and heckling you'd get thrown at you by the audiences but one day I found myself with no option but to do it.

As you will see within the next paragraph, I became a telephone engineer and I used to call into see my friend Adrian who had a printing business in Picketts Lock in Edmonton, which was on my patch almost every Wednesday morning around 10 o'clock for a coffee. One morning, when I walked in, I was greeted with "Here he is just the man." Now Adrian was chairman of an 'Old Boys Schools Team' by the name of Mayfield and they were due to have their annual presentation night on the coming Friday at The Chase Side Hotel in Enfield. Adrian told me that they had a problem whereby the 'after dinner speaker' had had to call off due to illness and asked me if I would fill in for him. I told him no-way, explaining my lack of confidence. He then put me into a really difficult position saying "If I didn't do it for him, he would have to postpone the event letting down 250 people" so what could I do? I reluctantly had to accept with him paying me what he'd have paid the original speaker, which wasn't a great deal, although my wife and I did get 'fed & watered' throughout the evening. I had no idea how to handle it but fortunately a friend who I used to sit next to at White Hart Lane had a father-in-law who at one time was an 'after dinner speaker' and latterly 'toastmaster.' He suggested I should go round to see him and get some tips, which I did. Norman was his name and he suggested that when I stood up, the first thing I should say was "Look, I've never done an 'after dinner presentation' before, actually that's not quite true, I have only once which was a 'Gay Dinners Night' a few weeks ago, so if any of you were there and have heard my stories, please be sympathetic to those here who weren't," which I received a good response for with it breaking the ice. I also went onto say, that I don't feel as nervous as I did when I arrived, as I got here a lot sooner than I intended, as I've had a few pints and I've loosened up, the reason being that I was driving to the event in my Red Ford Car and I was sitting at the traffic lights at the top of Kings Head Hill in Chingford, near to where I lived, looked in my rear view mirror and noticed this 'red' London Transport bus right 'up my arse.' As I came down the hill it was still right behind me and so I tried to lose it jumping some red lights and junctions at speed in doing so but it stayed with me all the way, only for me to find out when I arrived at the venue that I'd left my (red) boot open.

I have to say, the whole evening went down really well and it was a great experience and I'd love to do it regularly but you do need a lot of material and as I said before, be able to handle yourself with the hecklers. Although I did once have the opportunity of doing stand up. It was back in the mid 90s. I, my friend Barry, his friend Peter who feature 'heavily' in the next couple of paragraphs and another friend of their's went to Highbury to see us play the Arsenal. We were getting a right tonking 3-1 I think, it was with about 20 minutes to go when we thought we'd had enough of it and decided to leave the ground but before we jumped onto the tube home we decided that we would experience some of the great pubs that were situated around the Islington Upper Street area near to the Highbury ground. After going into a couple of pubs, we ended up in the Camden Head which was in Camden Passage. I was almost 'holding court' reeling out jokes whilst standing at the bar when a lady behind the bar, who seemed as though she had something to do with the running of the pub and on hearing my jokes invited me to do a 10 minutes or so stint upstairs at a 'stand-up' gig that they held on Saturday nights, whereby comedians trying to find their way in the comedy circuit got on stage and did a bit.

As said, I really did admire 'stand up' comedians and I remember a story I was once told about the comedy duo 'Mike &

Bernie Winters.' They were brothers, real 'old school' comedians, very popular performing between the 1950s & 70s. Mike was the older brother 'straight man' of the two, as there always was and Bernie the one who got the laughs. Actually they both came from Stamford Hill in North London, with Bernie being a massive Arsenal fan. They were appearing at the Apollo in Glasgow, by all accounts a venue that always gave comedy acts a rough ride by the audiences. As the older element of you reading this book will no doubt remember, Mike would come on first and do his warming up introduction bit, being joined a few minutes later by Bernie. As said, Mike was the straight man and was already getting some heckling from the no doubt it being in Glasgow inebriated audience, not being at all funny but then Bernie appeared from behind a curtain, showing his protruding teeth with this horrendous grin he'd put on, associated with a weird noise that that he'd make coming from the back of his mouth. It was a real trademark of Bernie's that made many laugh when he appeared but on one occasion, a punter sitting at the rear of the auditorium who obviously hadn't bought a programme and having no idea who was appearing on the night and not knowing who Mike & Bernie Winters were, took umbrage to it and on seeing him bellowed, in a Scottish accent "Fook me there's two of 'em,"

I was encouraged by my friends to go upstairs at the 'Head' as the pub was known to a do stint but luckily, the guy who was with us that I didn't know, said that he had to be back home in Enfield at 7.30 as he'd arranged to take his wife out for dinner, so with the gig not starting till 7.30 itself and it now being 6 o'clock we left, so who knows what might have been?

My second option of employment other than Charringtons, was to join, as it was then, the GPO, later to become BT, as a telephone engineer. Dear old Bill Bedford as previously mentioned, suggested I should work for them as he did, as they were very sympathetic with employees who needed time off to pursue their interest in sport as, as I said I did to get off midweek to play away games for then as it was Leyton in the Athenian League. Bill had contacts in 'high places' with the company and helped with me getting a job. This choice of employment was also my mum and dad's, as they liked the idea of it coming with a pension which I wouldn't have got at Charringtons, which I have to say at my age now I am really grateful for.

The GPO/BT themselves in those days had area competitions in London for football, tennis & cricket and it was not long after I joined that I got asked to play for the North London area football team. There was a lot of jealousy amongst other employees towards others who got selected to play any of the aforementioned sports as they'd get off work at noon or earlier sometimes if you were playing away. It was ok for home games but sometimes if you were away, you wouldn't get home until say 8 o'clock in the evening.

I remember one time we, North London, were to play South West London at I think it was Croydon Amateurs ground. Diagonally, I don't think you can get two areas of London further apart, pretty much North East across to South West. It was a freezing cold February day and we all had to meet up at Telephone House Crouch End in Hornsey at 11 o'clock. It was snowing, not heavily at the time but because it was in the days before mobiles, the guy who was running our team telephoned their guy to see what the weather conditions were like over there. He said that there were flakes of snow but it wasn't that bad, so we set off in our coach across London. The snow was getting worse and worse and when we arrived at their venue, there was a layer of about six inches on the pitch. So, the game was called off and we went into the bar to have a few drinks and bites to eat that were prepared initially for when the game finished before we set off back home. We were all at one end of the bar with the South West team at the other end but word had soon got round that they had a fella named Eddie Reynolds that was going to play centre-forward for them, who we'd all heard of who was drinking with their team. Eddie, was a colossus of a man who played for, amongst others, Wimbledon's amateur side with his claim to fame being that he scored four goals with his head in a FA Amateur Cup Final v Sutton United at Wembley in 1963. In a way we were glad that we didn't play the game, well, at least I know our centre-half was.

I also loved a game of tennis and I was fortunate to be asked to represent the area side at that as well. There were six of us in the team, three pairs of doubles and you played three games each consisting of three sets, all you were asked to do was to beat your opposite pair and the ones beneath your level then you would win the 'rubber' as it was known as. So the guy that I played, with, whoever it was, was only expected to beat their third pair as that was the level that I always played at, the third pairing.

As said, it was an area competition that we played in that you got time off work for but the GPO/BT did organise a London doubles competition that employees could enter albeit in 'their own time.' The idea being, that the winners of the London competition would progress into larger area competitions, ultimately into the national final.

Myself and a friend Barry, who was pretty much a reserve for our North London area tennis team, teamed up and got drawn against a couple of lads from Croydon. They contacted us and asked if we could play them on a Wednesday night at 6.30. at their club. Barry and I were what was known as 'subs apps' (subscribers apparatus) engineers, and we worked longer day hours into the evenings with the idea being that we had more chance of people being at home after work so that we could get into their homes to remedy their phone problems. Because of this, we got a day off every fortnight and arranged for our day off to be the day of the arranged tennis match. Barry lived in

Enfield and I at the time in Buckhurst Hill, which was at one time in Essex but moreso North East London then. We decided that it would take us both round about the same time to get into Liverpool Street 45 minutes, me on the Central Line he on the overland train from Enfield Town. We both set off at 3.15 to meet at Liverpool Street at 4 o'clock as arranged, then proceeded to walk along Bishopsgate then across London Bridge to catch the train to Croydon, albeit stopping in a couple of pubs on our way as it was a really hot summers day. On arriving at Croydon at about 6 o'clock, we were met by one of the pair of lads that we had been drawn against and whisked off in his car to their tennis club arriving about 6.20 to get changed and to get onto a booked 'grass' court to play at 6.30. So, three and a quarter hours to get there, three and a quarter hours to get back home, that by my reckoning was a round trip of seven hours. We went on court and lost 6-0, 6-1 in 25 minutes coming off at five to seven, what a fucking waste of time!

Barry was my trainee at B.T. and consequently we became very good friends to this day. Sadly, his lovely wife Lyn died a few years ago now but in the early days of their relationship Lyn got a bit frustrated that he hadn't proposed to her having lived together for some time. So Lyn thought she'd take it into her own hands to seal their fate. She phoned me one evening to say, "Can you send me a list of the dates that you and Barry have off" referring to Barry and I sharing the same day off that we did with what B.T. called the nine day fortnight that we worked, as explained in the previous paragraph. She said to me, that on the basis I spent a lot of time with him, I, as much as anyone would know how he would feel if she arranged a registrars wedding as a surprise. I told her that I didn't think he would be angry about it, so she went ahead and did it on the next Monday that we had both off together, which was a few months down the line as the days sort of ran consecutively e.g. Monday one fortnight Tuesday the second fortnight and so on. Lyn booked it with the Enfield Registry Office nearby where they lived, so all it took for me to do was to get Barry there with him not having any suspicions as to what was going on, which was even more difficult given that he had to wear a suit. Another good friend of his Peter had a plumbing business, so together we decided that we'd make out that Peter had been invited to a sort of 'Plumbers Awards Dinner' to take place on the afternoon of the arranged wedding at The Chase Side Hotel close to the registration office and that he could take one friend along with him and asked Barry if he would go, telling him it was a 'shirt and tie job' but enticing him by saying that there was going to be a comedian doing the awards.

So on the day, Peter went to pick Barry up but saying he had to call into the registrars on the way to pick up a copy of a birth certificate for his daughter which she needed to renew her passport with as she'd lost it.'

Luckily, there were a lot of 'double yellow'lines around the registration office to prevent Peter from parking his car so he had to park it some distance away. He called Barry's bluff, by asking him if he wanted to stay in the car or go with him to the registration office adding that it may take a little while, so Barry fortunately said he'd go with him. Myself my wife, Lyn and all of the other guests were waiting at the top of the stairs being as quiet as we possibly could. When Peter and Barry entered the building and got to the top of the stairs where the service took place, I walked out with a big red book and in my best Irish brogue a la Eamonn Andrews, I 'jumped out' and said, handing him the book, "Barry Clarke, you thought you were going to a 'Plumbers Award Dinner' but you're not, because this afternoon 'THIS IS YOUR LIFE' as within the TV programme that Eamonn Andrews was the first to present. He was shaken to his boots but everyone there thought it hilarious all except the registrar who wasn't so keen on it, as in her words "I've never experienced anything like this before." She did take Lyn & Barry into an office and in effect interrogated them as, as she explained, "These services weren't to be taken lightly as they were legally binding on a par with a church service." She did eventually go through with it and it all went well and we all went to a pub afterwards and celebrated and I think Barry was even pleased that it all happened.

I stayed at BT for 23 years and had some great times there, you were pretty much your own boss being out on the road all the time with no-one looking over your shoulder and the social side was brilliant to. I hadn't been there too long when I went on what was then called a 'Beano' outing, a 24 hour trip to Le Touquet in France. We set off in twelve coaches from Edmonton telephone exchange with some of the guys taking their musical instruments to set up a band on the ferry from Dover over to Calais. It wasn't a very nice day at all and we were warned that it would be a force 8 gale that we would be going over in on the ferry. It wasn't noticeable when we set off but as we got out of the harbour we really felt it. The band got set up and started playing with the drummer chasing his symbols all over the place as the boat rolled from side to side. I never did have good sea legs as they say, even though I was in the Lifeboys when I was young, their headquarters being up an alley way behind a church adjacent to Haringey's Sports Hall opposite the old Bell and Hare pub close to the Spurs ground, the pub incidentally, where Dave Mackay used to sit on the bar in the 'Snug Lounge' holding court with the rest of the Spurs double winning team drinking around him after a home game, that is except the captain Danny Blanchflower who didn't drink or socialise with them that much.

Back to the Le Touquet trip,. I spent most of the journey as low down in the decks of the ferry as I could, as someone told me it would stop me from feeling sea sick. We had some crazy people on the trip, with some dressed up in all sorts of fancy dress.When we got to Le Touquet, I remember one of our crowd looking into a restaurant through a window with a Wrigleys Spearmint packet on his shoulder, no not a small one, the bloody great big one that was used in the TV ad. We spent the afternoon in Le Touquet pretty much in the bars to keep out of the rain, setting off in the coaches to go back to Calais about 5 o'clock to catch the ferry back to England but when we arrived in Calais there was chaos. The weather had got considerably worse, the gale now being of a force 11 maybe 12 and to make things worse, one of the English ferries had sailed into the outer wall of Dover harbour which made the English ferry companies postpone theirs for the rest of the day. The French ferries were still operating but only from Calais to Folkestone not Dover, where we set off from in the morning, which led to a problem with some on the trip as they'd decided to drive down to Dover to meet up with us there, so somehow, they had to find their way back from Folkestone to Dover to pick up their cars. The other issue at the time, as they don't exist anymore, was that many on the trip had what were called 24 hour passports, so by definition, they had to be 'deported' from France back to England that same day, so although the ferries had in effect been reduced by half due to the English ferries being cancelled, our coaches took preference over any other vehicles that had people in them returning from holidays who had normal passports. It was now about 7 in the evening when we started going through customs and I was in the queue next to one of our crowd, he being dressed from top to toe in a Coldstream Guards costume, busby et al, in which he had four packets of 100 cigarettes hidden away standing upright in the busby. The funny thing was though, he had a ventriloquists dummy with him dressed exactly the same. The French customs officer asked the fella if he had anything to declare and the fella just looked at the dummy saying "I don't know, have you anything to declare?" The dummy replied by the fella throwing his voice "No, I haven't anything to declare." The customs officer being confused and taken by surprise, had never I assume experienced anything like it before, started having a conversation with the dummy and asked HIM if he was sure. In the end the customs official just let the fella and the dummy through with his packets of cigarettes still under his busby. We entered into the embarkation area where we told that our ferry wouldn't be leaving until 11 o'clock, maybe even midnight, so the lads set up the band once again to entertain everyone, we also opened up our duty frees that we intended to take home, so by the time we did board the ferry we were well gone. Myself and my friend Micky Eason who I was with, were supposed to be playing for Bill Bedford's (remember him earlier?) Sunday morning team the next day, so we had to phone him from a phone box, as you did in those days, to warn him, that we may not be back in time or in a fit state to play. Just before we boarded the ferry, someone suggested, given that we'd consumed an immense amount of alcohol, that when we get on board we should make our way directly to the restaurant to fill our stomachs to prevent us from being affected by the swell of the boat. A few of us were first in the queue, so we got our food and sat down and proceeded to eat it. Whilst we were, the boat started to set sail and again, similar to the journey over to France in the morning, it was quite calm and we were wondering what all the fuss was about, until we got out of the harbour. The force 11/12 gale was a lot worse than it was in the morning which really made the boat roll from side to side. Some people were either in the food queue or had just got theirs and were making their way to a table but the lurching of the boat took them one way with their tray of food going the other, to be honest it was quite scary with a lot of people getting thrown against the restaurant walls and getting badly injured. By then we had finished our meals but it was too dangerous to stand up let alone vacate the area, we just sat there hanging onto the leg of the table that was bolted to the floor, our chairs kept slipping and sliding but we just kept pulling ourselves back to the table by pulling on the leg. We were sitting quite close to the entrance of the kitchen when a guy, who turned out to be the restaurant manager appeared and stood above me yelling "El restaurant es ferme, el restauarant es ferme!" I looked up and responded "It may be 'ferme' matey but il es dangereux." With that, he grabbed me by the shoulder pad of my jacket and lifted me out of my chair still yelling that the restaurant was 'ferme.' To keep upright I just hung onto the lapel of his jacket and there we were hanging onto each other, until a fist came over my left shoulder and landed right on his nose which exploded with blood like oil coming out of a well. With that, a number of chefs appeared from the kitchen to assist him. It all got a bit ugly with skirmishes breaking out in the restaurant albeit there weren't many punches thrown, as anyone involved in the skirmishes were being thrown all over the place by the roll of the ferry, actually it was like a scene from a 'Carry On' film.

Eventually it all calmed down when the Captain and 1st officer came to see what the hell was going on. Actually, we were exonerated from any blame as there were some 'senior' BT people with us in the restaurant at the time and took our side, explaining to the Captain what started it, that being the restaurant manager being rather vociferous and to a degree physical albeit on me.

Working as a telephone engineer had many privileges going into houses/flats owned by many actors, singers and sports personalities as I covered pretty much North London with Hornsey/Crouch End, Highgate & Hampstead where many of them lived being a part of my patch.

I worked in Keith Moon's flat in Highgate Village, although he wasn't there at the time, in fact he hadn't been there for some time by definition of all the dogs pooh that was on the carpet that was rock solid.

I met the cricketer Leslie Compton, who had the Prince of Wales pub in the village and the Beatles manager Brian Epstein who lived in a flat in a mews behind the Starting Gate Pub in Highgate at the top of Spaniards Lane that winds itself down to Hampstead. Half way down Spaniards Lane to the right was Coniston Avenue, where I had to go once at 8 in the morning as my first call, where I went into the house of Lulu with no make up on, not me her, I think it was at the time she'd just parted company with Maurice Gibb he of the Bee Gees.

I also went into the properties of Alfie Bass, he of the Army Game and being a Gooner (Arsenal fan) as were The Kinks, whose recording studio I worked in in Tottenham Lane Hornsey. Hornsey, started to become a very desirable area to live in, in keeping with Highgate & Hampstead, albeit the 'trendy's that started to live there began to call it Crouch End in order for it to lose its identity as an ordinary part of Haringey the borough of which it was in. Someone told me a story once about Bob Dylan who decided he wanted to buy a house in England after meeting Dave Stewart of The Eurhythmics in the U.S. More to the point, he decided he wanted to live in England in Crouch End where Dave Stewart lived. The story goes that Bob flew over to England to stay at Dave Stewart's house whilst house-hunting in the Crouch End area. He went to a large Victorian house and rang the bell and an old lady came to the door. Bob asked the old lady if Dave was in but she replied "No. he's just popped down to the newsagents to get some cigarettes but would you like to come in and wait for him?" Bob entered the house and the old lady showed him into the front room and bought him a biscuit and a cup of tea in one of those little 'twee' cup and saucer, with the same printed design around the top of the cup and around the edge of the saucer. Not long after, 'Dave' returned with his cigarettes only to see the iconic Bob Dylan sitting in his front room but alas, it wasn't Dave Stewart it was some other 'Dave' and Bob had gone to the wrong house but what an experience it was for the other Dave albeit not for the old lady his mother as she didn't have a clue who the visitor was.

Four other memories of celebrities that stood out whose houses I worked in were the wonderfully charming Judith Chalmers, the radio/TV presenter who lived in a house in a Tudor type complex down Highgate West Hill that went from Highgate down to the Roundhouse rock venue, Warren Mitchell, who as everyone knows was a massive Spurs fan albeit with his alter ego Alf Garnett in To Death Us Do Part being a Hammers fan. Warren told me, that he gave up his season ticket with Tottenham because, although he had been a season ticket holder for many years, when he had to have two hip operations, the club wouldn't allow him the use of the 'Executive Lift' to get up to where his seat was high up in the old West Stand, he'd have to use the stairs which in the end he couldn't, which left him really sad and with a bitter taste in his mouth with regards to his supporting the club over many many years.

The best experience I can recall though in meeting a celebrity, was having to go to the house of the great Spike Milligan. I was in the hallway of his four storey house in Finchley attending to his phone, he being up as it turned out on the top floor that he used as his office. There was a ring at the door which his wife answered. Standing there and don't forget this was pre-mobile days, was a telegram boy, who handed a telegram to her. She opened it having closed the door and walked back to the kitchen, whereby she said to me, "Look what the silly old buggers gone and done now, he's sent a telegram asking for a cup of tea and two sugars." Brilliant.

Every year, us engineers would have to attend one of two GPO/BT colleges to be 'brought up to speed' on new telephone systems that that were being brought out. One of the colleges was in Old Street near Liverpool Street and the other by Kew Bridge, which was our favourite to go to just to see Concorde come into land at Heathrow Airport which was just up the road, as it would use the Thames as almost an extension of the flight path. At the lecturers annoyance, we'd all jump up and run over to the window during a 'lesson' when it came into view, as we were on the top floor of the building and we were almost level with the plane being able to wave at the pilot.

As you can imagine, because there were so many telephone engineers in attendance at any one course, many of them like myself had a story to tell about whose house they'd been into, especially those who worked around the Virginia Waters in Surrey area, where they'd entered the homes of celebrities such as Bruce Forsythe, Ronnie Corbett & Jimmy Tarbuck but the best tale that I can remember was one guy telling me that he had to repair the phone of Joan Collins. She had not long parted with her husband the singer and actor Tony Newley and she lived in a flat in Finchley which had a Highgate/Hampstead STD code. He said, she invited him into her flat and pointed to the phone that was situated in the hall on a shelf, which is where many phones were in flats in the day. He said, she told him to get on with what he had to do, saying that she was late for an appointment and needed to jump into the shower. By all accounts, the phone was on one side of the hall on the same side as the entrance to the bath/shower room but on the other side of the hall, was a mirror that reflected another in the bath/shower room, that in turn reflected Ms. Collins in the shower in all her glory. Whether she left it open for his benefit he wasn't certain but either way, he was able to witness what a wonderful figure she did have.

I also once, had reason to visit a house in the Muswell Hill/ Bounds Green area right behind Alexandria Palace where they now hold the darts tournaments. Alexandra Palace, which was at one time being discussed as to being the shared stadium of where Spurs and Arsenal were going to play, until the comedian Peter Cook being a massive Spurs fan, suggested on a London Weekend TV programme at the time that the ground would have to be fumigated after every game the Arsenal had played there.

I knew it was going to be someone interesting who lived in the house that I had to go into behind 'Alley Palley', as there was a big black Austin Princess parked outside. I have to admit, at first sight when I rang the bell for the door to be opened I didn't recognise the tall moustachio'd gentleman who opened it but on entering and then starting a conversation with him he turned out to be Tom Keylock The Rolling Stones Chauffer/Road Manager at the time. It was a very interesting couple of hours I spent with Tom, what with all the stories he told me. He was telling me that once whilst driving The Stones, the Austin Princess was nearly turned over by exuberant fans as they surrounded it and took me outside to show me the indentationed damage done to the vehicle whilst he was chauffeuring them around. I suppose meeting Tom was even more interesting to me, being a massive Stones fan at the time, as I'd been to see them a number of times including seeing them at The Regal Cinema in Edmonton as I said earlier in the book in 1965. I was telling him, that I once saw them in a small venue in South Tottenham called The Noreik, it being called by that name as the Irish owner had a daughter by the name of Keiron so he just turned her name around to give the venue its name. The venue, that was at the Tottenham end of the Seven Sisters Road by the junction of the High Road was at one-time a cinema named The Corner House, to which my dad took me to see, I think it was, the old Charlie Chaplin film 'Modern Times' which featured the song 'Smile.' written by Chaplin.

Tom told me that it was a matter of coincidence that The Stones appeared there, as it was recommended to them by a Greek tailor by the name of Nino, who had a 'bespoke' clothing manufacturing shop in nearby West Green Road where all the fashionistas at the time of the area including the Stones drummer Charlie Watts who it is rumoured lived in nearby Palmers Green at the time went to have their jackets and flared trousers made including me.

I also saw The Stones 'free' concert at Hyde Park in 1969, in fact there is video footage of me somewhere standing in the wings of the stage, getting access to it at the invitation of Tom Keylock having sorted out his phones.

Another Rolling Stones football related anecdote, was when they played at Wembley Stadium in the early 80s. and on the same night the England football team were playing a World Cup or Euros tournament game against some country that I can't remember maybe Ireland. I chose to go with a friend to the Stones concert rather than stay at home and watch the England game on TV. I remember England losing 1-0 and the Stones were late coming on stage having watched the England game to the end on TV at the back of the stage. The score was announced to the crowd in the stadium with The Stones coming on stage at the same time with Mick Jagger straight away breaking into 'You Can't Always Get What You Want' which was quite apt.

As well as the Stones 'free' Hyde Park concert a year after I went to another 'free' Hyde Park concert, anything 'free' and I was there. Among the acts was the band 'Heads, Hands & Feet' which at the time, had amongst it's members the wonderful Chas Hodges. The main attraction though were The Small Faces and during one of their numbers, a big fight broke out just in front of the stage. Stevie Marriott stopped the song he was singing and broke into a self made up blues type number singing "All you people out there, what are you fighting for?" Which stopped the fighting instantly with everybody cheering and clapping what he'd done.

In terms of the most nicest of people I had the privilege of meeting whilst working for B.T., I've left the best to last, it being the wonderful gentleman and violinist that was Yehudi Menuhin.

I introduced myself at his door as a telephone engineer to repair his phone system to which he replied, "Come right in Sir" I think I said to him at the time "I'm not worthy Sir." He was a really lovely gentleman. The house was opposite The Flask pub in Highgate, which he sold to Sting who in turn sold it to George Michael, it was the house that was in many of the newspapers that showed it with flowers outside when George died.

I also covered the Palmers Green/Winchmore Hill area where many of the Spurs/Arsenal footballers lived where I visited the premises of the likes of Frank McLintock, who lived in Wolves Lane Palmers Green, another real gentleman albeit a Gooner of course, that said, I'm being a touch hypocritical here as I was extremely grateful for a friend of mine who arranged for my now wife and I the chance to live in the flat of the old Arsenal right back John Devine when he wasn't there, as we were pretty much homeless at the time.

Another interesting road in Winchmore Hill was Broadwalk, that many christened 'Millionaire's Row,' where I worked in the house of the singer Frank Ifield, he with the yodelling voice of 'I Remember You' fame or 'I Remember You, You Bastard' as I prefer to call it, that said there were others who lived there at the time the likes of the comedian Ted Ray (No relation to me by the way), Rod Stewart before he moved out to Virginia Waters, the guy who owned Lesney's Matchbox Toys whose surname was Smith and Adam of Adam & the Ants, it was also rumoured that Paul McCartney had a house built in the road but never moved in.

I remember one Monday back in 1985, I was working in Palmers Green, in a complex of blocks of flats just off of Hedge Lane. I got out of my van to go round the back of it to get my tools and as I did so to my amazement, I saw the old Spurs centre forward Bobby Smith coming out of one of the blocks pushing a bicycle, with his decorating tools hanging over the handlebars which is what he did when he packed in football. There was no-one around, we exchanged greetings and then I took the opportunity of having a chat with him opening it up by saying, "Great win Saturday Bob" referring to Spurs beating Liverpool at Anfield for the first time since 1912 the year the Titanic sank, with Garth Crooks scoring the only goal which I witnessed by going to the game. Bobby replied,

" Yeah, but we wouldn't have had to wait that long to beat them up there if our Double side had have played them," following it up with "As Liverpool weren't in the first division then" as they weren't, they never got promoted until the '62 season. Bobby went onto say "Do you know what? I never played at Anfield, as they were in the 2nd Division when I was at my peak and then directly they got promoted, I got injured which pretty much put paid to my career." I remember Bobby having a knee injury and that Billy Nick replaced him, because of the uncertainty of him playing in the future, by buying Laurie Brown from Arsenal, who was ostensibly a centre-half that Billy Nick wanted to convert into a centre-forward. As it turned out, he wasn't any good at either. The story goes that Bobby wasn't best pleased and went into Bill's office to tell him so. An altercation ensued and it was said that Bobby leant across Bill's desk and grabbed him by the collar saying and referring to the signing of Laurie Brown "Are you taking the piss out of me?" Soon after Bobby was off loaded to Brighton and never played for Spurs again. Actually Tottenham getting in Laurie Brown for Bobby Smith wasn't the only bad piece of business between us and the Arsenal. 'They' always seemed to get the 'rub of the green' when it came to players who played for the two clubs. For example, we swapped Jimmy Robertson for David Jenkins, what was Bill Nicholson thinking of? Albeit I think that something happened with Jimmy Robertson within Tottenham F.C. that made Bill have to do it. We also 'let them' have Willy Young and Sol

Campbell amongst others, not to mention the debacle that was the great Pat Jennings.

I was also lucky and privileged as a telephone engineer, to be allocated a job to install an extension bell in the conservatory of Bill Nicholson's house where he lived in Creighton Avenue, a part of White Hart Lane, as White Hart Lane itself came up from the High Road and veered right at the junction of Creighton Avenue to go behind Tottenham Grammar School which was opposite to where Bill lived and then to come out at the other end of Creighton Avenue to continue its journey up to Wood Green.

I had a quick chat with Bill when I arrived but not for long, as his phone rang with Alan Mullery being on the other end of it telling Bill that he had pulled a muscle in his back whilst he was shaving of all things.

Bill was livid as Alan was the Spurs captain and they had an important game the next day against West Ham. Bill stormed out of the house and made his way by foot to the ground approxiamately two miles away in the High Road, which evidently he did quite often for his daily exercise. I was carrying out the installation of the extension bell when Darkie, Bill's wife, who was always seen riding around the Tottenham Streets on her 'midwife's' bike with a basket on the front, asked me if I would still be there when Bill got back for his dinner, as he always did at 1 o'clock, to which I replied that "I'd be finished before that." Darkie then produced a ten shilling note that she said Bill had left her to give me should I have finished the job before he got back. I was grateful and somewhat surprised, as Bill, being a dour Yorkshireman, had a reputation for being frugal with money. It was once said when he had virtual control of the club, that one night, when Tottenham had an F.A. Youth Cup match, he only allowed for the 'Mens' toilet in the West Stand enclosure, which was the only area of the ground open, to be open as it was necessary to have an attendant in it and he didn't think it worth it to pay a lady to be an attendant for the 'Womens' toilet, I don't know what the ladies did if there were any there that night if they wanted to visit the W.C.

Incidentally, I still have the ten shilling note to this day and proud of it. Going back to Billy Nicholson with a story I was once told concerning money, Phil Beal, the one-time centre back of Spurs went into Bill's office asking for a rise in his salary. Bill agreed to pay him something extra at the same time asking Phil to promise him that he wouldn't tell any of the other players, as it would make him the highest paid player at the club. Phil said he wouldn't but on a pre-season tour shortly after, Phil and the players were having a few drinks which made the 'old tongue loosen' and Phil let it slip that indeed Bill had granted him a rise in his salary and that he was the highest paid player at the club. I think it was Ralph Coates who said, "The bastard." Phil thinking Ralph was aiming the expletive at him replied "Who me?" To which Ralph said "No Bill, he told me exactly the same and asked me to promise not to tell anyone as well." Typical Bill.

There were many perks in being a telephone engineer, you could meet so many interesting people and work in many firms and factories that could be a benefit to you in what they did or manufactured. For a period, I looked after the telephone system installed within the offices of Tottenham Hotspur F.C. and on one occasion, it would be around 1968/9, I was in the main office remedying a problem with their system when Mike England and a couple of other players came in and collected brown paper envelopes from a lady that was in there, the envelopes I can only imagine containing their wages, oh how times have changed. Myself and my friend Micky Eason had tickets that were given to me by Tottenham's club secretary, I think his name was Peter Jones, in appreciation of me looking after their phone system for many years to see the Spurs v Arsenal game played on a

Monday night in the 1970-71 season, with all Arsenal having to do was at least get a draw to win the double. There were so many people outside the ground prior to kick off, some say as many outside as there were in it. Mickey and I got trapped up against the gates that led into the club offices in the High Road. It was ridiculous, you just couldn't move and our tickets were for seats in the opposite East Stand. Luckily, the secretary who gave me the tickets came out of the offices and noticed me and opened the gates just enough to let us squeeze through. When we got in, the secretary pointed across the car park to a door and said "Go in that door and if anybody asks you're mending the phones in the press box" which the door led to. He then went onto say, "When you get into the press box, you can jump over the wall surrounding the pitch and walk round to the East Stand and walk up into your seats" which luckily we were able to do. Mind you, that was one perk I didn't enjoy, Ray Kennedy scored a goal that gave the Arse a 1-0 win which won them the double and all on Spurs own soil. Sickening!

As I said, I needed to get a job where I could get off early from work especially in midweek when we played away, as was the case when I played for Leyton in the Athenian League, so I joined B.T. I was asked to sign by the Leyton manager at the time a chap by the name of Eddie Gray, not the ex-Leeds winger or the one in the 'Crazy Gang' the comedy act that included 'Flanagan & Allen' though another one. I signed around the March time with a view to me replacing their top goal scorer a lad by the name of Jimmy Green who was going to turn professional the following season with a club that I can't remember. Jimmy was a great character and took me under his wing, I was only about 19/20 at the time. One Thursday evening after training, he asked me what I was doing the next night, it being a Friday. He said he was going to the Blues Room, a venue for rock bands situated above the Manor House pub close to Finsbury Park and asked me to join him. At the time there were many 'small venues in North London like the Blues Room where you could see bands for about 5/10 shillings in pre-decimalisation days, places like The Cooks Ferry Inn by the River Lea in Edmonton & The Klooks Kleek, which was above the Railway Tavern in West Hampstead which were my favourite haunts. You could see the likes of Roxy Music and Long John Baldry's 'Steam Packet,' that featured Rod Stewart and The Brian Auger Trinity whose lead singer was the beautiful Julie Driscoll whose single 'Wheels On Fire' was the theme tune for Absolutely Fabulous. The other venue I used to enjoy going to, although it was some distance from where I lived was on Eel Pie Island an actual island on River Thames where I once saw The Rolling Stones for about the same money. Just think, 5/10 shillings and how much are fans paying now to see Rod & The Stones near to £100, mind you I suppose it's all relative in terms of wages as they say. Incidentally, just to digress, Eel Pie Island was where Trevor Bayliss the inventor of the 'wind up radio' lives.

As said, Jimmy invited me to join him at The Blues Room but the problem was, it was a regular haunt for me that I went to every Friday night with a group of friends. I told Jimmy this, also telling him that I would have a word with them to see if they minded. He said well, "If you can make it I'll be outside the entrance at 7 o'clock." I thought it would get me some 'browny points' by meeting up with him, so I told my friends what was happening and along I went to meet Jimmy as he wished. He was really pleased to see me and he said "Right let's go in." I led the way and proceeded to go round the corner into Green Lanes to get onto the end of a queue that was about a quarter of a mile long and getting longer. As I did so, Jimmy asked me where I was going, to which I replied "To the end of the queue," to which he replied "Nah this way." We went straight up to the entrance doors where there were standing a couple of burly security guys who greeted Jimmy with a "Good evening Jimmy welcome."

Jimmy said thanks and introduced me to them as his pal Johnny Ray. They greeted me in the same way they did him and we made our way up the stairs to where the club was. Again, I led the way to turn left at the top of the stairs into the bar where the stage was, as I would do every Friday night, only again for Jimmy to ask me "Where are you going.?" "To the bar I replied" to which he responded by saying again "Nah this way" and banged on the what looked like an oak panelled wall on the opposite side of the top of the stairs but it wasn't a wall as such, it was a panelled door leading to what can only be described as a 'snug bar.' Again, a burly security guy opened the door/panel and let us in saying "Evening Jimmy." Again Jimmy said, "This is my pal Johnny Ray" culminating in the security guard in saying "Welcome Johnny come on in." We made our way to the bar only to be met by none other than Pete Townsend, John Entwhistle, Keith Moon and Roger Daltrey who were playing there that night in their early days maybe as The Who or as in their former name The High Numbers, either way I was flabbergasted, I don't think I muttered a word in awe. Mind you, if only I knew then that Roger Daltry was a Gooner.

I hope it wasn't down to me but the Leyton manager Eddie Gray left soon after I signed, taking up a similar post at Dagenham before they became Dagenham & Redbridge. Eddie was replaced at Leyton by a great character by the name of Ronnie Duke, who was a type of guy you couldn't wait to go into training to be with he was so funny. I think that's the thing with managers/coaches like that, they are real characters the likes of Ronnie, Terry Venables, Malcolm Allison, Ian Holloway and of course Harry Redknapp, they are characters who you couldn't wait to go into training with they are a joy to work with. I remember us at Leyton playing in a cup quarter final once when we had a couple of 'tiny' guys up front and the ball was kept being played up to them in the air which they had no chance in competing for that made Ronnie at half time bellow "What's the point of pumping balls up in the air to a couple of fucking Charlie Drakes." For those who don't know, was a comedian of the 60s extremely vertically challenged. I did actually put the same question to Terry Venables in a question and answer session at a shareholders meeting at Spurs, albeit using Nico Claesen and Clive Allen as the players in question who were also on the shortish side. Also, Leyton's ground, situated behind the Hare & Hounds pub in Lea Bridge Road, wasn't the most salubrious of places, as many amateur grounds weren't at the time. I remember one Thursday night we had a power cut at the ground and the communal bath, that was allowed at the time until AIDS came along, had about six inches of luke warm water in it but we didn't have any lighting either, so Ronnie our manager, went out into the street, gave two lads a couple of bob each to get them to come into the changing rooms so that they could stand their bikes up on their rear wheels so that they could rotate the pedals with their hands to get the dynamos going to work their headlamps so we could get some light in the rooms and just to think, I thought I'd leave playing football in the Banks League where Lloyds Bank's football team had underfloor heating in the dressing rooms to better myself to play in the Athenian League in such other salubrious venues as Epping Town, Cheshunt, Bishops Stortford, Tilbury & Walton & Hersham amongst many others

THE HALF-TIME QUIZ

To while away the time with your Bovril & meat pie

1. Who played for Arsenal in the morning and Tottenham Hotspur in the afternoon?

   Ans. The Band of the Metropolitan Police

2. What would the decision be, if a keeper took a goal kick and the ball goes out of his area but a massive gust of wind blows the ball back over the keepers head and goes into the goal?

   Ans A penalty to Man. Utd.

3. What would it be if a players goes down the wing, crosses the ball and it lands on top of the crossbar on top of the near post then rolls along the crossbar and stops dead in the middle of it?

   Ans. A bloody miracle

4. How do you know when Man. United are at home?

   Ans. The M5 is chock-a-block.

Tottenham's 1960-61 'Double' winning manager Billy Nicholson, holding open the gates of the main West Stand that we used as a goal when we used to play a game whilst we waited for the players to come out from training so that we could get their autographs. The other goal, was between the two white barriers that came down the steps from the West Stand in the background.

Baronet Road where I lived. The pillar on the corner is all that's left of the lamp post, the base of which we used to play cricket. In fact it would have been better as it is.

Me and my friend Barry, the one we organised the surprise wedding for, with the 1981-82 F.A. Cup at Spurs old training ground at Cheshunt.

That's me in the middle of the back row left of our keeper Chris Whitbread as you look at the photo when I played for Cheshunt United, with our charismatic manager and wonderful guy Bill Bedford and Private Walker of Dad's Army lookaloke at the end on the right

Ossie Ardiles & Ricky Villa outside the quaint old Antwerp Arms by Bruce Castle Park, the pub that my friend Chrissy Lane was instrumental in retrieving it back to a Communiy Pub popular with the Spurs fans at the top of Church Street right opposite the Park Lane End off the new stadium, taken on the day of the last game played at the old White Hart Lane

The sad and decrepit sight of what was The British Queen pub which is a few hundred metres from the old White Hart Lane ground where I and many of the Spurs players of the 60s & 70s spent many an hour drinking

Eat your heart out Richards Osman.

That's me, 'leaning' on the cross bar of a set of rugby posts and watching the planes come in at Stanstead Airport. I was always a 'tall' lad for my age.

A few years ago I designed a range of novelty football greetings cards, examples of which are on this and the following pages

HE'S MISSED IT
AND HE'S GOT HIS
HEAD IN HIS HANDS

"THEIR WINGER'S ON FIRE"
8
FIRE SERVICE
FIRE SERVICE

HE'S SOLD HIM A DUMMY !!

SECOND HALF

Leyton and I parted company when I was in my mid-twenties. I had some great times when I played for them and although I was grateful for the 'expenses' I got each week that subsidised the wages I was getting from B.T. which weren't great to say the least, I got fed up with the competitiveness of the football and the ritual of training every Tuesday & Thursday nights and the travelling, even though it was relatively local it being the Isthmian League with matches being played around London and I suppose the fact, that although Leyton had been successful in earlier years, they weren't whilst I was with them, what does that say?

So I decided I wanted to give 'it' up and watch my beloved Tottenham Hotspur, or play in local junior football with my friends when Spurs were away, not that I didn't make friends at Leyton, I did and they were great guys, not least Jimmy Green as within the aforementioned The Who story.

I had a lot of 'not-drinking' time to make up for as well because of the training and forfeiting the opportunity of going to my favourite haunt Dingwalls in Camden Town on a Friday night because I'd be playing on the day after. So, I did start going to Dingwalls again finding myself standing in a queue on occasions behind the likes of John Oates of Hall & Oates and the actor

David Carradine, who I remember had a ruck sack on his back. I had a Ford 1600E Silver Fox at the time, with there only being a limited edition number of them being made. I met a girl in Dingwalls one night and asked her if she wanted a lift home, which she accepted on the condition that I took her friend as well. When I left the club with the two girls on my arms, we walked to where I knew I'd parked the car but it wasn't there. I started to doubt myself as to where I'd parked it so we walked around the adjacent streets to see if we could find it somewhere else albeit without success, with the girl I'd offered the lift home to saying "Come on be honest, you haven't really got a car have you?" I was so keen to get my wicked way with her that we hailed a taxi as I thought if I'd reported the theft there and then I'd end up down the nick for a few hours giving a statement and blow the chances of my sexual intentions.

As I said earlier in the book, I was living in a house in Highbury Fields at the time, with three girls and a friend of mine Micky. Micky had not long been banned from drink driving and when walking home from work one evening, not only did he make the observation that 'roof tops were beautiful,' something you don't notice when you're driving, he found my car parked up behind Highbury Corner Underground Station about a week after it had been stolen, with its' radio and steering wheel taken with the wheels luckily still intact. We informed the police and they took it to Camden Town Police Station for fingerprinting. They released the car about a week later but before I could collect it, I had to replace the steering wheel, so my friend Micky took me to a Ford dealer in Wood Green to get one. As we were driving back to Camden Police Station to replace the steering wheel and collect the car on the following Saturday morning, along a packed with shoppers Wood Green High Road, Micky was driving with his steering wheel and I had my replacement one in front of me on the passengers side as if I was driving as well. You should have seen the people peering into the car, they couldn't believe what they were seeing, they must have thought it was some sort of futuristic type of vehicle.

The Monday week after retrieving the car from the police station, I left the house to go to work about 7.40.a.m. somewhat bleary eyed, as I'd had a drink the night before at the Torrington on Tally-Ho Corner in East Finchley where we used to see live bands every Sunday night, bands like Osibisa and Kokomo. As I pulled out from outside my house where I was parked, I set off but as I did so, a car pulled out from between other parked cars about 100 yards ahead of me that were left there by commuters to catch the tube into the city from nearby Highbury Station. Because there was only enough room for one car to travel along the road because of cars being parked either side of it, I slowed down to let the oncoming car come between mine and the last commuter parked car to my right but instead of the oncoming car veering over to pass me it come right up to the nose of my car. The four doors of the car flew open, with some big burly fellas leaping out of it, one of them coming round grabbing hold of my arm through my window as I'd opened it to enquire as to what was going on. They said to me, that they were police and that they knew the car had been stolen to which I replied, "Yes but I got it back some ten days ago" to which they replied "Yeah, how many times do you think we've heard that one?" I didn't really know what was happening and didn't know if they were police or not until I got bundled into the back seat of their car where there was a policeman's uniform and helmet stacked up and with an Alsatian dog barking at me from behind a grid from the rear, which made one of the 'old bill' say in an arrogant manner "Don't get too near the dog son, he hasn't had his breakfast yet." They took me to Highbury Station where it transpired that when the car was released by Camden Police Station, every other London police station was notified except Highbury as their computer was down on the day. It made things worse as 'they' had been staking out the house where I lived since the Thursday before and knew of every minute of when I'd been at the house or stayed out for the night, so they'd had to have been there 24 hours of four days completely wasting their time and the tax payers money.

Throughout the 60s/70s & 80s, apart from having our football club, Tottenham was a great place to live if you were in your teens or 20s. We had The Tottenham Royal, which we frequented on Monday, Thursday & Saturday evenings standing at the bar next to the ladies W.C. witnessing every girl that was in the establishment on the basis that almost all of them had to visit it at some time and to where I could walk to and walk home from was The British Queen, which has sadly closed down now. It was a few hundred yards from the old Spurs ground which backed onto the railway line that served White Hart Lane Station. You could socialise with many of the Spurs players of the late sixties and early seventies in there, the likes of Phil Beal, the two Martins, Chivers & Peters, Terry Venables and Joe Kinnear, who I personally got quite friendly with probably due to the same hairstyle of the time that we had. The guy who owned it was an Irish guy by the name of Vince, who was a real character who later in the 80s owned The Coolbury Club in Tottenham High Road where you could rub shoulders with Glenn Hoddle himself, Chrissy Waddle and Gerry Armstrong whilst at the bar after games and later, the Cross Keys that was on what was called Edmonton Green just north of Tottenham where the Migil Five, who had a No. 1 with Mockin' Bird Hill used to appear regularly on a Friday night.

The British Queen, or 'The Queen' as it was locally known, was the pub to go to and I almost 'lived' in there throughout the late mid to late 60's, and throughout the 70s & early 80's, it was buzzing almost every night.

In 1982, as I'm sure you'll recall, Dexy's Midnight Runners brought out the popular iconic record 'Come on Eileen,' in which in the opening line of the song I got a mention. It was obviously referring to the aforementioned one-time American pop singer of the same name, albeit with the spelling of his christian name for some reason being spelt incorrectly , it should have read JOHNNIE not JOHNNY as mine is. When the record was released, it was often played in the pub and when it was I would get virtually the whole pub, fingers in the air pointing at me with every man and girl singing it to me, which was quite endearing really. About 10 years ago, I went down to London to stay with a friend in Loughton but on the way when arriving at Liverpool Street on the train, I went to meet a friend by the name of Barry who I got to know all those years back when we used to drink in 'The Queen.'

At his request we met in the Cross Keys in Bishopsgate. The pub was an old Barclays Bank, very dark inside with a circular bar in the centre of it. As I walked round, not being able to pick anybody out in the darkness, I heard Barry shout out my name to which I responded to by going over to where he was sitting with his friends to give him a bit of a man hug. After about 10 minutes, his friends decided they were going over to another pub called The Lamb, that was situated in Leadenhall Market just across the road. Four of them got up and went that left Barry, another friend of his and me sitting there chatting. After a while Barry asked me if I fancied going over to The Lamb to continue drinking with his friends but I declined, as I told him I needed to be in Loughton at 5 to meet my friend who I was staying with, with the time now being just after 3. Barry tried to convince me by saying that there would be a guy by the name of Nigel in there who played guitar as a session musician with Dexy's Midnight Runners. I said what "On Come On Eileen?" He said "You've got it" to which I said "What the song that I get a mention in ?" Well with that, he and his friend almost frog-marched me across the road saying "Of course I forgot about that bit in the song, you've got to come and meet him." When we walked in, Nigel had his back to us and all I could see was his now bald head having got many years older since the record was released albeit I do remember him sporting a nice blue-petrol coloured leather jacket. When we walked in, Barry tapped him on the shoulder and said in his cockney accent "Oi, Nige, what was Dexy's all time best record?" There then followed a conversation that went something like:-

'Nige': "Best or most commercial?"
Barry: "Well most commercial then"
'Nige': "'Come On Eileen' of course"
Barry: "Who was it about?"
'Nige': "Johnny Ray"
Barry: "Meet JohnnyRay"

Nigel took one look at me and said "You're joking. Do you know what? It's 30 years since that record's been out and I've never met anybody by the name of Johnny Ray " and proceeded to get on his knees and started to bow down to me. I straight away said to him "Nigel, I'm not worthy" and helped him get up on his feet. He was a lovely fella was Nigel and we chatted for ages he telling me great and interesting stories about guitarists like Eric Clapton, Pete Townsend and others, albeit he did tell me that at the time Kevin Rowlands, the main man of Dexy's Midnight Runners was in some hospitalised premises in Sussex to help him get over some personal issues he had at the time, all very sad.

All this made me late for my meet up with my friend in Loughton and it didn't help that I had a quick walk around Spitalfields Market which I always love to do when I'm in the area. As I did, I noticed a guy there selling printed 'T-Shirts' on a stall and he had one on with 'I CAME ON EILEEN' on it, which I regretted not buying to this day, in fact, I was going to give this book that as a title but I was deterred from doing so by the publishers as they thought it may jeopardise the sales if any of the book.

Funny thing, I've instructed my wife to play 'Come On Eileen' at my cremation, as the opening line would be appropriate but even more appropriate on the basis it will be a cremation, might be Billy Joel's 'We Didn't start the fire' as 'I' get a mention in the opening line of that as well, along with Harry Truman and Doris Day, what do you think?

Mind you, my daughter asked what I wanted played if I were to be buried and I replied "Going Underground by the Jam."

That reminds me of the time that Bob Hope's kids threw a party for him for his 100th birthday and they asked him "Dad, what do you want to be when you die buried or cremated?" Bob replied "I don't know, surprise me." 'Genius.'

Very near to The British Queen was a teachers training college off of White Hart Lane. It was called All saints, in its early days an all girls college, the girls all coming from far and wide throughout many parts of the country. Many would go to The British Queen just to suss out the local male talent that was in there, which us lads benefited from, sneaking back to the girls rooms in the college unless you got caught which was very often the case. I have to say the name of the college All Saints being rather 'contradictory' given the behaviour of the girls that attended there.

This was all around 1967 and one night, I met a girl in 'The Queen' and went back to her room in the dormitory of the college avoiding the gate security and whichever lady college lecturer that was on duty that night to prevent any skulduggery going on with the students inviting us boys back to their rooms.

We had the pirate radio station Radio Caroline on whilst we were in bed which was at around 1a.m.,when it was boarded by the authorities and taken off the air, I tell ya, I loved listening to Radio Caroline, it was the only radio station that you could hear proper rock music on and I was so upset when it happened, I got out of her bed got dressed and went home.

A few months after in September of that year, the BBC launched Radio 1. It wasn't the same thing, the music was more 'poppy,' it being launched for the masses rather than the connoisseurs of rock music. The BBC even took the DJ's from the other main pirate ship at the time Radio London, which was also taken off the air around the same time, which again was more 'poppy' than Caroline. DJs that had been initially with Caroline, the likes of Tony Blackburn, Dave Lee Travis & Keith Skues all literally 'jumped ship' to leave Caroline to go over to Radio London. Mind you Caroline replaced them with arguably better ones who were more in tune with rock, they being the likes of Jonnie Walker, Tommy Vance, the wonderful gravelled voiced Mike Raven and Emperor Rosko, whose real name was Mike Pasternak the son of Joe the film director. Jonnie Walker was great, many couples used to sit on the cliffs of Frinton-on-Sea in their cars late at night when Jonnie's show was on looking out to where Radio Caroline was moored and Jonnie used to say to them over the air, "If you're in your cars on the cliffs of Frinton flash your headlights just the once but if you're being naughty in your cars, flash them twice" which many often did.

As said, Radio 1 was launched in September of 1967 with the first DJ to broadcast on the station being Tony Blackburn, his first record that he played being 'Flowers in The Rain' by The Move. I had an old Rover 100 at the time, a beast of a car that only did about 15mpg. It was a great car to get the girls into the back of, it also had what they called 'Suicide Doors,' those that opened opposite to conventional car doors as they had the hinge at the rear of the door rather than at the front of it as on the American cars that the gangsters always seemed to have in the films of the day. I remember one time sitting in the front seats of the car with a girl I'd took out on a date. When I got her back to outside her home she said to me, "Get in the Back" to which I replied "No." She again said "Get in the back" and I again said

"No." She asked "Why not?" To which I replied "Cos I want to sit in the front with you!"

C'mon these are the jokes folks.

On the morning of the launch of Radio 1, I was driving to work in the Rover along Tottenham's Lordship Lane. Tony Blackburn had on his programme, some may remember, a fictitious dog that he named 'Arnold' that would bark periodically in between records for some unknown reason. It was horrendous, so much so I decided to try and find an alternative station to listen to, a station with music more of my liking albeit without success. I did so, by turning the knob on my radio, as you had to at the time but whilst I was doing it, a young lady in an Allegro car in front of me admitted that she saw a work colleague of hers standing at a bus stop right outside Lordship Lane Recreation Ground. She didn't have time to pull right over to the kerb but she slammed on her anchors with her drivers side of the car still in line with my passengers side. We were in a steady stream of traffic and only doing about 20m.p.h. but 'bang,' did my car make a mess of hers, hers was like a bell tent with mine only suffering a dent in my front nearside wing albeit with a mini, driven by another young lady going into the rear of me, the young lady being one that I knew from seeing her often in the British Queen.

There was a police motor cyclist on the other side of the road passing by, who witnessed the whole thing and blamed me.

A few nights later, said lady in Mini came up to me in 'The Queen' and said that the police motor cyclist had called round her house to take a statement and afterwards asked her out and she asked me whether or not she should accept his invitation. I said to her to say to him "If you take the blame off of Johnny (me), then I'll go out with you" which he did and she did.

Unfortunately, the Rover didn't survive the crash, I got it to a friend of mine who was a mechanic who had a lock-up nearby and he diagnosed that a piston ring had gone on it and to repair it would cost more than the damage that it incurred. I scrapped it, my only regret being, that I didn't keep my registration number plate as the three letters that preceded the three numbers on it as they did then, were the same as my initials JAR 'John Alfie Ray,' registration plates not being as collectable at the time as they are now.

As said, All Saints Teachers Training College was initially an all female college but as time went on it was opened up to the male gender as well, albeit with the ratio of boys to girls being very minimal. The year before the males were invited to join the college, the females went on a what they called a 'field trip' to Brittany, with the only two males going on the trip being the coach driver and the college Bursar. Between them they had so much trouble keeping the local French lads from getting into the camp site with the girls, the following year males were invited and included on a similar trip, mostly to assist the Bursar from having to fend off the local French lads again on his own. By this time, myself and the lads from 'The Queen' got very friendly with a number of the new males that were now studying in the college, as they started to come round to the pub with the girls that we already knew. Now, I can't remember precisely how it happened but myself and another couple of lads from 'The Queen' got invited to go on the trip. The ratio of females to the men was quite high, it was a 62 seater coach, with 54 females and 8 males of whom only 5 were students and me and the other two guys from the Queen, oh yes and of course the Bursar. As said, it was classed as a field/education trip and we stayed in a camp site in Dinan/Dinard, a beautiful part of France and the world come to that and although there was a lot of socialising being carried out it was very 'educational' in the true sense of the word. We went to the Mont St. Michel and on another day to a castle/fortress on a north Brittany beach which was known as the 'Fort de la Latte,' which was featured in The Vikings film starring Tony Curtis & Kirk Douglas. As said, the whole thing was a 'great experience.'

A lot of the lads who drank in The British Queen, the Spurs players apart, were good footballers themselves and in the summer, during the close season when pubs used to close at two in the afternoon on a Saturday and when we weren't playing for our respective clubs, many of us used go off and have a kick about somewhere. We used to go to a school in the adjacent borough of Edmonton by the name of Hazelwood Lane. Now kids of a younger age won't remember this but in the day, if you were having a kick-about between two teams and you'd started, if say two lads turned up late, in order to decide which lad would join which team, it was decided by them both going, what was called 'pudding or beef,' one of them going pudding the other beef, then one of the captains would choose one or the other and the lad that was of that choice would join that captain's team. We had to climb over the railings of the school to play, as it was during school holidays and we were never prevented from doing so because, although the caretaker lived on the premises, he was always too scared to have a go at us but one day it happened, two coppers were striding across the green grass to confront us. As they got to one of the touchlines, Brian Ellerbeck, he the peanut seller at Spurs home games as mentioned earlier in the book, said to the two coppers, "Sorry lads, you'll have to go pudding and beef." We did get turfed off but we were back there the next week.

Another place we went to on Sunday afternoons when the pub closed was High Beech, in the middle of Epping Forest. It was a trendy place to be seen in the day but we'd still find an area of green grass where we could play a game of football and I remember some guy, who was a regular at 'The Queen' taking the opportunity of taking Vince the owner of 'The Queen' out of the game knee high and really injuring him, so much so, that

Vince barred him from the pub for some considerable time until he lamented.

In the late 60s, Spurs were drawn away to Everton in an F.A. Cup game at Goodison. A number of us who drank in 'The Queen' decided we'd go up there and somehow got hold of twelve tickets. Myself and one of the guys rented a twelve seater mini-bus from a garage in Palmers Green on the eve of the game which was to take place on a Saturday. We told everyone to be at 'The Queen' at eight in the morning and "don't be late." Of course there was always one, who we had to pick up at Enfield Highway on the way, a guy by the name of Johnny Leach who got a part in Eldorado the soap shot on the Costa Del Sol. I think he played a hit-man in it, shooting a guy by the name of Charlie if I remember rightly. As he was getting into the back of the van we were all shouting at him "Come on Leachy we're late." He replied, "It's alright, I've got my breakfast" holding up a bottle of whisky. With the palm of his right hand, he hit the screw cap on top of the bottle with the top spinning off the bottle and going about a foot into the air, as the top came down, he caught it and started guggling the scotch out of the neck of the bottle holding it with his left hand, it was so coolly done, James Bond would have been proud of it.

When we did meet up though at The Queen, although it was a twelve seater mini-bus and having the same number of tickets to get into the game, sixteen people turned up. It was impossible to tell four that they couldn't go, so we all piled in the van and off we went.

When we arrived in Liverpool, we parked up in a car park that was on the outside of Stanley Park that separated Goodison Park where our game was being played and Anfield, Liverpool's home ground. Now I don't know why the FA. allowed it to happen but on the same day we were playing Everton, Liverpool were drawn at home to Manchester City, albeit they kicked off at 2.45. and we at 3.15. As we were getting out of the van to put our coats on, two Liverpool fans appeared on the other side of the railings in Stanley Park making their way to Anfield. Now in the late 60s, although The Beatles had done their bit in lifting the profile of fashion in the north, it was nowhere near the level of fashion that the southern half of the country enjoyed, especially in the London area and to that end, you could easily identify which people came from which half of the country. It was like the Beatles/Stones thing really, if you were from the south you were generally a Stones fan but if you came from the north you were a Beatles fan. Anyway, these two lads came rushing up to the railings that separated us growling and almost frothing at the mouth, with one of them shouting in his Liverpool accent, "All you fookin' Loondoners are all fookin' queers" to which my friend Chris, or 'Rotters' as is his pseudonym on the Spurs Odyssey Forum, who was decked out in a three quarter length Prince of Wales check coat that tapered into his waste responded with his hand on one hip camp style, "Well some of us might be duckie but I can't speak for all of us." That made the Liverpool guy react even more frantically, almost trying to pull apart the railings to get at Chris. Chris had and still has a great sense of humour, he being famously known for wearing his 'Spurs' underpants with a cockerel on the front crutch part of them outside his jeans at the 1971 League Cup Final v Villa at Wembley.

We made our way to Goodison and when we arrived at the ground where we needed to enter, we all squeezed into the turnstyle as best we could throwing all the twelve tickets at the ticket collector simultaneously. He didn't know what was going on but we all got in. We rushed upstairs to our seats that our tickets were allocated for and took it in turns to sit down or move about going to the loo etc.

We won the game 2-0 with goals by Chivers & Alan Gilzean.

"Spurs were on their way to Wembley."

Luckily afterwards, when we got back to the car park, the two lads that we had been confronted by before the game were nowhere to be seen, so we got in the bus and decided to, rather than get beaten up in a Liverpool club that night by Everton fans whose team we had beaten, go to Manchester. We went to the Hacienda Club but when we came out to come back to London, we found the mini-bus's windows smashed in with many of our expensive fashionable London leather coats stolen. It was freezing driving home with no windows early in the morning.

Around the same time, myself my friend Micky (he of the Mickey Mouse' name giving fame), went up to Derby on the train to see a game. We played two games v Derby around the same time and we got hammered in both 5-2 & 8-2, this was around the time the Spurs hero Dave Mackay left to go to Derby as he was considered too old to play on for us. On the rail journey home from one of the games, the Spurs fans decided they'd take the 'heavy' defeat out on British Rail and proceeded to unscrew the light bulbs in the already darkened carriages as it was winter time and throw them out of the window, also, 'they' took a ladder from one of the carriages that was more or less a carriage where you could store bicycles and threw that out of the window as well, that I suppose could have landed on the other track going the other way, it was crazy and ridiculously stupid. We arrived at a station by the name of Ampthill in Bedfordshire where the police stopped the train. The train was too long for the platform to accommodate all the carriages, only the first half of them. Myself Mickey and a guy we were with who we worked with at BT, who was a family man his 50s, were in the nearest carriage that you couldn't alight from onto the platform. Our 50 plus year old friend against my and Mickey's better judgement, decided he wanted to speak to a policeman to see what was going on as he was expected home at a reasonable time by his wife and kids. He poked his head out of the window to shout at the policeman who told him to go through to the door of the adjoining carriage which was 'accessible' from the platform and he would speak to him which he did, with the policeman telling him to "Get off the train" which he pleaded against albeit to no avail. Mickey and I decided we couldn't leave him on his own so we went with him. While we were standing now on the platform, we asked the policeman what was happening and he told us that the rest of the train was being pulled up to the platform so that they could get everyone off it. So we stood there with the train starting to slowly go along only for it to gather speed and carry on it's journey onto Euston with the rest of the fans still on board. We were flabbergasted and we let the policeman know in no uncertain terms which he thought was hilarious. We started to make our way out of the station not knowing what to do seeing the rest of the fans up ahead of us only being visible in the dark by some roadwork lights that they'd picked up and were holding and swinging that they'd nicked from some nearby road works. Luckily for us, we hang around for a while and spoke to another policeman who seemed to take pity on us and told us to make ourselves scarce for three quarters of an hour until another 'local' train would come by so that we could continue our journey to Euston, albeit a little belatedly.

Oh by the way, Ampthill was only a small village with a post office and one pub in it, albeit we later found out with the pub being in a hell of a mess following the Spurs fans that had been thrown off the train taking their revenge out on it. Actually, Billy Nicholson decided to take a team up there shortly afterwards out of sympathy for the village and to raise money for the refurbishment of the pub.

A crowd of us from 'The Queen' used to go down to Torquay for Bank Holiday weekends to experience the taste of the 'Scrumpy' cider that was brewed down in Devon.

One weekend when we went, we arrived around six on the Friday evening. Me and my friend Mickey Eason having booked a B&B, were invited on our arrival to sit and have an evening meal with the owners and their children. Around the table we got talking to the patriarch of the family, with the conversation moving onto football. He said that Torquay were playing that Friday evening and invited us to go down to Plainmoor their home ground to see them play. Well thinking we wouldn't be going 'clubbing' til about 10.30. we accepted his invitation. We watched the 'dour' first half then went into the bar at half-time and didn't come out of it until after the game finished, completely as they say 'rat arsed.'

The following morning, our crowd of about twelve, met up and had a 6 a-side kick-about on Abbey Lawns, an expanse of parkland opposite Abbey Sands Torquay's main beach before the pubs opened. During it, two MGB convertibles turned up. The two lads driving them got out and strolled over to us. One of them, looking rather 'dapper' wearing a cravat said to us, "You lot look rather decent, do you fancy a game." We replied that we were due to be going back to London the Sunday evening the next day, so we said "Yeah we could but it would have to be on the Sunday morning, Perhaps after we could all go for a drink together" which was arranged.

After the kick about on the Saturday, we went into a pub where we stayed until 2 o'clock when it closed. It began to rain as we left, so not being able to go to the beach we took refuge in a café next door to the pub. We were all sitting around when we befriended this really funny Welsh guy who we nicknamed 'Ivor the Engine' after the childrens TV programme at the time, albeit his real name being Neil McCabe. As said, he was a great lad and would tell joke after joke. The first thing he said to us was, "I had a bit of trouble last night over there (pointing to the harbour). This fella was looking at me and said something, so I picked him up and threw him into the harbour and then I threw his wheelchair in after him." He then went onto tell a series of jokes, one of them being the first ever joke that I can remember and kept logged in my memory.

He said "This fella walks into a café and summoned over the waitress and asked for a cup of tea and then spouted out the letters "P.I.S.S." She ignored him and went to get his tea to bring back to him. He then asked her for a bacon sandwich and then followed that up saying the letters "C.U.N.T." Well that was that, the waitress called the manager and he in turn called the police. The fella ended up in court with the judge saying "Defendant, you've been charged with using obscene language in a public place, how do you plead?" The fella said "Not guilty your honour." To which the judge said "So what did you mean by these letters P.I.S.S. & C.U.N.T. and did you say them?" The fella admitted he did but still pleaded his innocence so the judge asked him to explain himself. The fella said "Well they're acronyms, I asked for a cup of tea, P.I.S.S. 'Put in some sugar.' The judge then said "And what about the C.U.N.T. with the bacon sandwich?" The fella said "Well that meant 'Cut Up Nice and Thin." So the judge said "Fair enough, I find you not guilty." To which the defendant said "Thank you very much your honour "And by the way, (spelling out) B.O.L.L.O.C.K.S." The judge said "And what does that mean?" With the defendant replying "BOLLOCKS."

'Ivor' kept us entertained all afternoon and I became very good friends with him. It turned out he was a massive Spurs fan, which was a bit strange he coming from Llantwit Major near Newport in Wales. I went to visit him sometime afterwards and coincided it with Spurs playing a pre-season friendly with Cardiff City. Ivor, now called Neil by myself, was very impressed that I was able to get free tickets off of Phil Beal who was playing for Spurs in the game, me getting them from him when asking him for them in the British Queen one night. Neil was even more impressed when we turned up at the players entrance at Ninian Park to collect the tickets at the players entrance when I introduced him to Phil, Joe Kinnear and Ralph Coates. I stayed with Neil for the weekend and on the Sunday morning I played in a doubles tennis match with him and two of his friends, one of them being the drummer of Andy Fairweather-Low's band Amen Corner who'd just had a hit with 'Wide Eyed And Legless.'.

The other thing that sticks in my mind with Neil, was when we went to a night club in Torquay and 'pulled' two girls. We were on the dance floor with them, with the one he was with wearing a long dress that at first didn't reveal anything but she then began to unveil the top of it by undoing a sort of scarf and revealing her boobs in all their glory, yes it was what they then called 'topless dresses.' Everybody else stopped dancing, there were only us four left on the floor. Mine didn't have a topless dress but she did have a well known name, it being 'Maxine Bygraves' the daughter of Max who had a home in the town and what a gorgeous looking girl she was too, it was a shame she lived so far away.

Perhaps I shouldn't give the guy 'the time of day' but here goes.

In Torquay, there was a hotel perched high up on a hill up from the harbour, it may have been called 'The Riviera' I'm not sure and when the pub we were in closed at 2 o'clock we went up there. We went through the hotel to the rear of it where there were a considerable number of steps that led down to a sort of concrete platform that skiers got into the sea from to be towed around by speed boats. It was a beautiful day and we sat on the platform chatting, sunbathing and just generally chilling out listening to music that we played on a wind up record player that someone brought along with them. A girl who was with us, was an off-duty chambermaid who worked in the hotel. As we were playing the 45 rpm records, she mentioned that Jimmy Saville was staying at the hotel, so we asked her to go up there to see if he would come down and join us. Off she went and soon there he appeared, in a silk type smoking jacket smoking one of his trademark cigars with a chambermaid on each arm, one of them being the girl we sent up to get him. He was standing at the top of the steps, so we beckoned him down to play some records for us which he duly did, introducing them with his DJ voice accompanied by that silly noise he made as on Top Of The Pops. Actually, he came over as a really nice fella but alas not as nice as we thought.

Anyway, back to the game that we arranged to play on the Sunday morning. There were still markings on the grass of Abbey Lawns as to where the pitch was when it was used during the football season but no goalposts but our opponents brought over eight corner flags that we used, four for the goalposts and four for the corners of the pitch. As I've said earlier, we did have some half decent footballers including the, at the time Finchley goalkeeper, a lad by the name of Johnny Burgess and Johnny Nash, not the singer but the father of STEVE NASH the very successful and wealthy American basketball player who I believe thought about buying into Tottenham Hotspur F.C. on a couple of occasions. Yeah, that's right, that's the connection between Steve and his love for the club, his mum and dad living for many years in Lordship Lane in Tottenham opposite Lordship Lane Recreation Ground where I had my accident in my Rover 100 car where they lived prior to them emigrating to South Africa where Steve was born before again moving onto the States.

We won the game 4-2 and when we moved into the pub afterwards to have a drink and a chat, it transpired that who we had just played was for the most part Torquay United, with the guy who came over to us to ask us to play being their centre-forward and top goalscorer Robin Stubbs who at one-time, was married to Anthea Redfern, the one-time wife of Bruce Forsythe. The guy in the other MGB being Tony Scott, the former West Ham winger. I remember him because I 'pulled his 'bird' when we went back down there a little later in the summer, she living in the adjacent town to Torquay of Babacombe.

Incidentally, Spurs had to go down there the flowing season having been drawn against them in the F.A. Cup, drawing 3-3 at Plainmoor and beating them 5-1 at White Hart Lane in the replay with Robin Stubbs in their team. Shame we couldn't arrange for them to come and join us in The British Queen after the game.

Football and music have always seemed to go 'hand in hand,' well they have in my world. In 1974, about half a dozen of us from 'The Queen' went to Wembley Stadium to see a concert made up of Joni Mitchell, whose act we only saw the end of because we were late getting there, The Band & Crosby Stills & Nash (Not Johnny, Graham) & Young. I was determined that I wanted to stand on the grass right on the spot where Ralph Coates scored the winner in the 1-0 victory in the League Cup Final v Norwich the previous season, which I did, albeit not on the grass but on the tarpaulin that was used to protect the pitch.

That said, we went to another concert the following year at the same venue, which consisted of Chaka Khan and some bloke in a blue shirt, white shorts and white socks that went up to his knees but could he play the guitar. They were followed by The Eagles, then The Beach Boys came on with Elton John the final act and supposed star of the gig. The guitarist in the blue shirt was good as were The Eagles but The Beach Boys were awesome. I remember it being a really hot day with wall to wall blue skies but so hot that Johnnie Walker, who was the DJ playing vinyl records on his decks in between the acts having to stop as the sun was melting the vinyl. That apart, it was great, the whole crowd were linking arms across the Wembley pitch swaying and singing the lyrics of California Girls by The Beach Boys. Elton John came on after at around 9.30. and he was a real let down after experiencing them so we left around ten to get to our regular Saturday night haunt that being the The Bull n' Bush in Hampstead/Golders Green that the song was written after, as we knew we would always get a party from there to go to until the early hours of Sunday morning, which we did.

Oh btw, the guy in the Blue shirt and white shorts was

_ _ _ _ 'Joe Walsh,' who later as we all know joined The Eagles.

When my wife and I moved to Norfolk I was asked to help in coaching the Norfolk Schools teams. We'd have two coaches coaching each age group in the event as much as anything, one of us weren't available for any reason. My colleague was a fella called Mark, a school teacher and he and his wife invited us to a friend of theirs birthday party in Harleston in Suffolk near Diss where he and his wife lived. I was told to wear a multi-coloured printed half sleeved shirt as it was a Californian themed party with a Beach Boys tribute band The East Coast Beach Boys performing. Now I've never been into tribute bands, I've always been of the thinking that 'if they're that good they should be doing their own thing not leaching off the back of others" but they were incredible, they played and sang just like them note for note, if you closed your eyes you wouldn't know it was a tribute band you'd think it was the real thing.

I still wasn't keen to go to see tribute bands but many years later, because my wife and I were great fans of theirs back in the 70s and as I've said before, I having seen them at the Finsbury Park Rainbow many years ago, we went to a venue named The Harbour Rooms up here in Blakeney on the North Norfolk Coast to see 'Steamy Dan,' yes a tribute band to 'Steely Dan,' the name given to the band by the founder Donald Fagan, it supposedly meaning in the 'states' a sex toy of sorts. Actually, I am intrigued as to how bands and artists get their name, did you know that Axl Rose the lead singer of Guns N' Roses got his from an anagram of Oral Sex? Steamy Dan were brilliant, they were a ten-piece band made up of three in the brass section, two female backing singers and five others that played guitars keyboards and percussion. As we came out of the venue there was a poster on the wall advertising another tribute band 'Oye Santana,' the real Santana being another band I saw back in the 70s at The Hammersmith Odeon as relayed in a following paragraph. My wife and I both thought that we may be missing something in our ignorance with our view on tribute bands, so we thought we'd go along to see them as well and they didn't disappoint, they also were brilliant.

I've also been a fan of Neil Young and we found out that the sound engineer in the aforementioned Harbour Rooms had he's own band by the name of 'Don't Spook The Horse,' a tribute band, again based up here in Norfolk to Neil Young & Crazy Horse, another great act that we've seen a number of times now.

Having seen these tribute acts has completely altered our view on them, most certainly if they are dedicated to bands whose lead singers have died and you'd never get a chance to see them again. Actually, I have a friend who lives in a nearby village from ours who has his own recording studio with one of Frank Zappa's old mixing desks in it. He has his own Reggae/ Ska band The Sweet Beats and have played at Glastonbury. I love talking music with him but I'm always wary in what I have to say because he knows so much more about music than I do and reluctantly, because I thought he might talk them down, I was always apprehensive talking about tribute bands to him. He and his wife got tickets to see Steely Dan in London about eighteen months ago, so I mentioned that my wife and I had seen the aforementioned Steamy Dan tribute band and the others but to my surprise he said that, instrumentally, the musicians in the bands are often as good as those in the real thing, the only difference being that they don't have the genius in writing the songs that the originals were famous for.

I have to say, North Norfolk has a vibrant live music scene, much more so than from what I've experienced when I have visited there of late rural parts of London, say Enfield or Loughton where all you've got is big burly security guards on the doors of pubs that there's no live music in monitoring who can and can't go in, albeit I suppose it may be different as you go more into the heart of the city e.g. Camden.

In Aylsham, which is only a couple of miles from where we live, there is a pub The Unicorn that I've mentioned before that has 'live' music every Friday and sometimes on a Saturday & Sunday (that should see me ok for a few pints from Will the landlord in the future). Also, again a couple of miles from us is a drinking establishment by the name of The Gunton Arms, with articles on it often seen in the 'full'scap' newspapers. It is owned by a guy by the name of Ivor Braka, who is known to move in celebrity A-List circles being an art dealer with Bryan Ferry it is said, being one of his top clients. There are many examples of the works of artists like Damian Hirst and Tracey Emin on display in there, some of them a bit 'naughty' with regards to Ms. Emin's works. It is situated in a massive estate with it, back in the day, being a place that Lilly Langtree would frequent who allegedly had an affair with King Edward VII, they may have even stayed there together who knows? On a hot sunny day there is not a finer place in my wife and I's opinion in 'the world' where you can sit outside supping a pint and watch the deer grazing, I have to say, without being patronising to Ivor I trust, we are truly grateful for him giving us such a place to socialise in not least being able to rub shoulders with many celebrities and musicians who also frequent the place and stay there., A couple of years ago, Take That stayed there following their penultimate gig of their U.K. tour, it being at Carrow Road, Norwich City's ground, in fact, they had their end of tour party there not least because I understand it's one of Mark Owen's favourite places to frequent.

A couple of years ago, my wife and I got the nod from someone who's 'in the know' there, that a helicopter the size of a Chinook would be landing there on a Sunday afternoon and that we should go along to see who it was who was in it. We did, to witness members of Pink Floyd and Genesis alighting from it, not that they were recognisable with their now shorter hair, if they had any at all and their 'conventional' clothing that they were wearing.

The Gunton, throws an annual music concert in the grounds every August, well they did until all this corona virus malarkey took hold, not holding back on the economics of organising it either, with a massive marquee in the grounds bringing up bands from London. So, that's another pub I'm looking to receiving free pints from the owner from for advertising.

There was a situation with regards to music and 'The British Queen.' I bought ten tickets to go and see Santana, as I said in the previous paragraph at the then named Hammersmith Odeon before it became the Apollo. Eight of the tickets were for four couples, me and my young lady and three of my close friends and theirs. I bought another two just in case and I sort of half promised them to another guy and his lady albeit he was unsure whether or not she wanted to go. On the Friday night on the eve of the concert, in 'The Queen,' I was approached by a guy by the name of Dave Cook who was renown for being able to look after himself also being a Taekwondo instructor. He said that he'd heard that I had a couple of spare tickets for the concert, to which I replied "I have Dave but they're promised to someone else" to which Dave replied "Well, has he told you that he wants them?" Well he hadn't, I could have been stuck with them notwithstanding that I didn't want to say "no" to Dave, so I let him have them. Luckily the other guy never came back to me.

So off we go to Hammersmith to see the wonderful Santana the next evening. We had eight tickets in one row with Dave and his young lady in the row behind us at the other end to where I was sitting. I kept looking over my shoulder to make sure he was enjoying himself as he hadn't offered me any money yet for his tickets and I thought there was more chance of me getting some if he was. With about 15 minutes to go of the concert, Santana broke into 'Jing-Go-Lo-Ba,' their big hit and everyone in the auditorium got onto their feet to dance to the music. Again, I looked over my shoulder only to find Dave and his lady not being in their seats, so naturally I thought 'fuck it,' there goes my money, he's walked out. Then as I looked back to the stage, there they both were dancing in the wings, how they got up there I never did find out. The following night Dave came up to me in "The Queen' waving some banknotes and said to me "How much do I owe you Johnny? That was the best night I've ever had." I told him how much and he gave me the money and then he went onto say "And I've told Vinnie (the owner), that you've not to pay for any drinks that you have tonight they're all down to me." Result!.

After the 71-72 season it wasn't a good time to watch Spurs, what with Billy Nicholson resigning, things started to go downhill, so I started playing on Saturdays for various clubs. Bill Bedford, who I'd played for before in the Walthamstow U-16 League, re-formed a team to play in the Hertfordshire League retaining the name Cheshunt United (the name not to be confused with the actual Cheshunt amateur team) the name he called the team a few years previously when he got us altogether as youngsters having been too old to play in the U-16 Walthamstow League. We'd all grown up by now and we were a good side and could have given said Cheshunt a run for their money. I also turned out for All Saints Teachers Training College that I mentioned earlier was an all girls college with many of the girls frequenting The British Queen. By this time, the college had become a mixed college of males and females with the males forming a football team, playing other colleges throughout London. I used to play as what was named a 'ringer' not being a student of the college, I got asked to play as I spent a lot of time socialising in the college, as I'd been going out with a student for some time that I met at 'The Queen' by the name of Gilly .

On our first date, I took her to an up-market restaurant whereby I had the lobster and she had chicken breasts and frogs legs but she had a wonderful personality.

Only joking!

Actually the first date I took her on, we went in my old Rover 100 that I had the accident in to a nightclub that was very trendy and popular at the time in Woodford, Essex called The Kingfisher. We spent the night with Terry Venables and Graeme Souness as they were with a guy I knew by the name of Gyppo, a local popular Tottenham lad and a good dancer often seen at the time on the TV music programme 'Ready Steady Go' who invited us over to have a drink with them.

Gilly I suppose, was the first real love of my life and we were in a relationship until we had to decide whether or not it was going to be a long term thing or not, as we came from two completely different backgrounds, me coming from a working class family, my mum being a factory worker at the London Rubber Company, which was handy for condoms for my dad and he being a night-time bus cleaner for London Transport, Gilly came from a family of wellbeing, her 'father' being a chief executive for a well known 'grass seed' company. I think a lot of it was down to me and my complex about the situation, it was like the forerunner to the BBC drama 'Normal People' where Connell's mum was the house cleaner to Marianne's well to do mother.

Not long after we split up, Gilly graduated from the college to become a teacher and got a flat in Hampstead. She'd have these short term relationships with other fellas but when they didn't work out she'd phone me and ask me to go over and see her and empathise with her which I always did.

The only thing that really riled me, was when she was about to leave the college and they had the annual May Ball. I was all set to go with her but at the very last minute she dumped me to go with some bloke by the name of Ernie, who had pots of money but looked as he sounded. I was so annoyed, so to get my own back I left a message in her pigeon hole at the college to say that Ernie had been called away up to Lytham St. Annes urgently on business and that she was to call him before five in the afternoon. On calling and asking to speak to 'Ernie,' she was answered by some bloke saying "Very funny, how many calls do you think we get like this a day?" Yes I'd set her up, it was ERNIE (Electronic Random Number Indicator Equipment) the Premium Bonds line.

Gilly eventually went back to Ipswich where she originally came from and met up with an American guy who was known as 'Buddy,' his real name believe it or not being George Washington, a really cool dude who was stationed in the American Air Force base at Woodbridge close to Ipswich.

I was living at the time with three of Gilly's ex-All Saints College friends in the big old house on Highbury Fields, the house that I mentioned earlier in the book when I had my Silver Fox 1600E that was stolen from outside Dingwalls . There were five of us living there, myself, my friend Mickey and the three lovely girls. It was a great place to live being just up the road to Upper Street in Islington, great I say, until the wind blew up the wrong way from Arsenal's Highbury Stadium. We used to have regular on going conversations out of our upstairs window with Arthur Mullard the 'comedian,' who lived over the other side of the fields with his sister, who used to stop to get his breathe on a bench opposite our place on his way to The Cock pub by Highbury Station.

As said, it was a great place to live, not least being to the north 'The Rainbow,' a great rock venue of the 70s in Finsbury Park where at the time you could go to see two concerts a week which we often did, seeing there the likes of David Bowie, Little Feat, The Doobie Brothers, the wonderful Steely Dan lead by Donald Fagan, which not many people had the fortune to see and the original rock opera of 'Tommy,' starring Roger Daltrey, Peter Sellers as The Doctor, Tina Turner as The Acid Queen and Keith Moon who played the type casted 'Mad Uncle.' I remember at the time 'Loons' type trousers were all the craze, now how do I explain them for those who don't know? They were two toned, very often the top half being beige and the bottom dark brown, with the two colours meeting at the knee in an 'apex' format like the top of a triangle/pyramid but what were Keith Moon's made up of? The bottom half were of the dark brown material but the top half being his beige coloured skin, with the top of each 'apex/pyramid' being tied by string or something up to his underpants that were visibly on show for all to see, completely 'mad,' as we all knew he was in the nicest possibly sense.

The Rainbow, was formerly known as The Finsbury Park Astoria which was ostensibly a cinema, albeit they did have occasional pop/rock concerts there in the 60s., even having The Beatles perform there. In 1971 it became purely a rock' venue, the interior décor being something else. As you went into the round foyer, which was quite a size, there was a beautiful fountain, with the bar just to the right of it. In the auditorium itself, there were balconies high up on the sides of the inner walls where they met the ceiling, that were in effect Spanish hacienda type buildings, making it look like a Spanish village all discreetly lit up and I remember the ceiling being black, with white stars painted on it, it was just like watching a concert 'al fresco' especially as said, with the haciendas all around the adjoining walls.

Unfortunately, the venue didn't last that long, it closed in the mid to late 70s I think because of the sound damaging the structure of the building. The thing is, it is a Grade II listed building so it can't be knocked down and is now being used as an Evangelical Church.

To the south of the house that we lived in, there were some great pubs to frequent that we often did. We had The Albion in Barnsbury Square, The Compton Arms in Compton Mews, the Rising Sun in Brookeby Street, in Upper Street there was the Hope & Anchor, which was great for live music in the basement, the Kings Head, which I don't know if it still has, an old-fashioned 'till' to keep the money in that had the old pound shillings & pence signs pop up when you pressed the keys to insert the money, the Camden Head in Camden Passage and behind Camden Passage down by the canal, the great boozer that was the Island Queen, that had paper mache dolls, one of which was 'sarcastically dedicated to ' Maggie Thatcher perched on top of a cupboard that was in an island itself behind the almost circular bar holding up the optics, a pub where you could often sea George Best (more of him later) with the actress Sinead Cusack, who lived close by as they were an item at the time.

Incidentally, the house we lived in on Highbury Fields was once used for the contestants in The Apprentice. One of the girls that I lived there with told me recently that she was offered the opportunity of buying it for £30k, this being in the 70s, what must it be worth now, £1.5m?

The aforementioned Gilly, often used to come down with Buddy to visit us and come to our parties, I really got on with him even though he knew of mine and Gilly's previous relationship. I returned the compliment once by going up to visit them, mainly because I wanted to go and see Spurs play Ipswich. I went up by train from Liverpool Street, went to the game and then went to their flat where I stayed the night. We were all supposed to be going out clubbing on the night but Buddy for some reason decided he didn't want to go, so Gilly and I went on our own which was bit bizarre, it was just like old times.

After some considerable time, their relationship fizzled out. I don't know why, whether it was to do with him having to return to America or with her family not approving of their relationship, who knows?

Buddy obviously 'held a torch' for her for some time, as one night some time later, myself and some friends went to the Ipswich Gaumont to see a popular rock band of the time named 'Man' and because Gilly was living in Ipswich she came with us as we had a spare ticket.

We went in a couple of cars, me being in my friend 'Fudgie's' with his then girlfriend. We went to pick Gilly up on the way and on returning from the concert for some reason, we stopped off at her sisters to pick something up. On arriving, her sister said to Gilly "Don't take Johnny round to your flat because Buddy is there waiting for him with his American pals from the base, all supposedly armed with appropriately baseball bats. Gilly suggested we should drop her off at the bottom of her road but being the big hero, I didn't want to let her go on her own, at the same time not wanting to drag my friend Fudgie into it. In the end we did what Gilly suggested, she saying that he (Buddy) wouldn't hurt her. I must say, I didn't take that much persuading.

In the summer of that year, my friends and I decided that we would take three weeks off work and drive down to Morocco, albeit renting a flat in Los Boliches in Fuengirola down on the Costa del Sol for one week before we crossed the Med to go down to Marrakesh for the second week and then back to the flat in Los Boliches for the final week.

Gilly decided she wanted to come with us, albeit being the only girl as she'd 'had a shit year' and she wanted to get away for a break. All my friends loved her, so there was no problem as far as they were concerned, not least she evened up the numbers so that we had three in each car. We left my flat in Highbury around two on a Saturday afternoon and made our way down to Calais to get across to France to then drive down to Spain. The idea was that the lads in the other car would do a 'stint' of four hour driving, four hour sleeping then four hour navigating and again four driving again and so on. In our car it wasn't as easy as that, as Gilly wasn't insured to drive Fudgie, my friend's car which was a company car, so he and I had to do a four drive stint then have a four hour sleep with Gilly doing the navigating which she couldn't do all the time as she had to sleep. We stopped in Spain at about 1.a.m. to have something to eat and then continued our trip. We were high up in the mountains around four in the morning, when I was driving and I was feeling really tired. I flashed my friend Terry who was driving the car in front to let him know. We were stopped opposite an all night café/bar so we went over to have a coffee leaving the others asleep in the cars. We had a chat and decided, that if I was still feeling tired by the time we got to the next town, we would stop for a real break. Next thing I awoke with the car embedded into a tree. The car was in a mangled mess with Gilly next to me squashed up against the dashboard. I could see smoke coming out of the bonnet and managed to get a pair of scissors from her hand bag so that I could cut her seatbelt and get her out. This all happened as I said, high up in the mountains, outside a beautiful hacienda type of dwelling which had three Mercs in the drive, a swimming pool and tennis court. When my friends in the car in front realised that we weren't with them, they turned around to find us on our knees on the side of the round which must have been a real shock to them. This was all pre-mobile days and they tried to stop what cars there were coming passed at that time of the morning, albeit as they thought without success, so one of them ran into the grounds of the hacienda banging his fist on the wooden shutters of the windows shouting, "Accidente, Accidente," The lights came on one by one with someone eventually coming out saying "No telephono, No telephono." All that luxury eh but no telephone. Someone who was passing in a car must have taken notice, as a police/ambulance jeep came and took the three of us to hospital. It was only that we were all asleep that we weren't that seriously injured so we were told, albeit if I hadn't fallen asleep it wouldn't have happened at all. Gilly was the only one of us that really needed treatment. Fudgie and I just had bad bruising to our ribs and legs, so they kept her in for 48 hours and we went and stayed in a hotel. When she was discharged, the three of us got a train down to Malaga where we were picked up by one of our friends in what was the only car that we had between the six of us, how we arranged it I can't remember, as, as I said, we didn't have mobiles to speak to each other on. Obviously, the part of the holiday to Marrakesh was off as we only had the one car, so we stayed in the apartment in Los Boliches. What with what had happened and I suppose the six of us in one apartment, it all got too much, especially for Fudgie, who was obviously distraught about his car and left for England after only a few days and it was too much for Gilly, who was still in a lot of discomfort, so she and I got a tickets and flew back to England where we were met by her mum & dad at Heathrow.

Well, if her dad didn't think I was good enough for her back in the day, he certainly didn't think I was much cop now having nearly killed his daughter. I think this was what really finished any relationship that we may have had in the future.

Going back to the 'ERNIE' story involving Gilly. I later had a relationship with another girl that I went out with who'd been a student at All Saints Teachers Training College who had moved into a flat in Golders Green with some of her mates. When I arrived there to pick her up on a date, the music from the flat below was blaring out, so much so that you could hardly hear ourselves talk. We spoke about it and although the girls had asked the fellas in the flat to turn it down previously, they were completely ignored, so we decided that we would make out we were Golders Green Police Station and called them to say that we'd had some complaints and to save time wasting on the police's behalf in coming out, would they kindly respect other people in the flats and keep the music down, which they did, with no further problems. (Impersonating a police officer, moi?)

With the above in mind, I told the girls of a programme that I'd heard on the radio called 'Does The Team Think?' One of the questions that the panel were asked was, "What was the naughtiest thing they ever did when they were kids?" Arthur Askey the comedian was on the panel and replied, "I and some friends went into a telephone kiosk once, looked up the name 'Smelly' in the directory and phoned one of them up saying when the call was answered "Are you Smelly?" To which the recipient of the call replied, "Yes." Arthur Askey then went onto say we said, "Well then get a bath" and dropped the phone and ran as fast as they could away from the phonebox as if they could have got caught.

The girls loved the idea of doing it but I declined, I wasn't in the mood at the time. Two days later, I went to the flat to pick her up again, only for the girls to say "Guess what happened last night ? We had a dinner party, got a bit tipsy and decided that we'd do what you said about Arthur Askey." They went onto say, that they phoned the first number which was unanswered, then the second number only to be told by the person answering the call that Mr Smelly wasn't in but when they made the third call, on it being answered they said "Are you Smelly?" Which he answered in the affirmative only for the girls to shout down the phone "Well get a bath then" only for the Mr Smelly to reply ""FUCK OFF!"

Around this time I turned out to play football for Air France. My friend Tony, who I got nicked with for avoiding paying our train fares when we went to Upton Park, as told earlier on in the book, worked for them and along with his work colleague Johnny Waring, who had played for a number of South London amateur teams including Tooting & Mitcham and Croydon Amateurs, organised matches between their Air France office in Bond Street and other Air France offices throughout Europe and beyond. I used to go up and meet them and their other work colleagues, especially a guy by the name of Johnny Marriott, who just loved modern jazz and knew every jazz club in London, in a pub that was behind their offices in Bond Street. I can't remember the pub's real name, we called it 'The Jaws Of Death' One of the regulars to be seen in there was the 'Carry On' actor Kenneth Williams, whose raucous loud voice you could hear over everybody else's. I don't know if Johnny Marriott was an Evertonian by birth but he was a big Everton fan. He once went to Stamford Bridge to see his beloved Everton play Chelsea. Everton went 1-0 up which made a Chelsea fan shout out "Come on Chelsea, you can beat this rubbish" to which Johnny Marriott replied, in a scouse accent, "C'mon the roobish." Anyway I digress, back to the football. Air France once played as far afield as Rio de Janeiro against the Air France office there but I wasn't allowed on the flights for the long haul games, although I did get to play in Brussels, Monte Carlo and Paris, the latter on a number of occasions. In fact, I don't think I saw the Eifel Tower for many years of going to Paris, as we would always socialise after games with a spread laid on in their offices in Montparnasse, or we'd go to the restaurants in the African Quarter and then onto 'Harry's Bar,' never taking on any sightseeing.

Over the years, I became very friendly with the guy who organised the Paris Air France office football team by the name of Patrick, who also held a high position in the company.

He once invited me to play for the Paris office team against IBM one Friday evening in Paris, which coincided with me going on a ten day holiday the following day to Sicily with him and three of his friends. His three friends and I drove down but Patrick flew down with my friend Tony who also came, as they got free tickets from Air France as employees of the company. We won the game 4-3, with myself scoring a hat-trick. It was bit embarrassing really with Patrick telling the opposition that I was on Tottenham's books and he'd got me over to play, which of course I wasn't.

We set off the next day, it was a wonderful journey down to Sicily, driving from Paris and taking in beautiful cities such as Grenoble, Genoa, Pizza, Rome & Naples, then to the foot of Italy where we got the ferry over to the Sicilian town of Messina. The only problem was though, was that we'd driven the 1.5 thousand kilometres down there and when we rolled off the ferry in Messina, Patrice, who was driving the car, went into the back of the car in front causing both cars a bit of damage that we had to get repaired before we could continue our journey. All that way and then that.

We stayed on the island for ten days, in the home of Patrick's friend Enzo Sezzari. Enzo was a wine merchant but seemed to have his fingers in so many pies.' The following evening Enzo, drove us to Palermo airport where we had to pick up Patrick and my friend Tony. We got about a couple of miles from the airport where we got caught up in a traffic jam that turned out to be a 'police stop check' which happened quite frequently what with the mafia and all that. Enzo must have been very well known on the island, so much so that we were sitting in the queue of the 'stop check' when a policeman came along and shone his torch into our car. He straight away recognised Enzo and asked him what he was doing. Enzo told him we were picking up friends from the airport, so the policeman summoned a police motor cyclist to escort us all the way down the middle of the road to the airport to meet Patrick and Tony on time, which we wouldn't have done without his assistance.

It turned out that apart from Patrick and us being invited down there for the holiday, Enzo wanted to pick Patrick's brains as well, as by all accounts, Patrick once managed a nightclub in London's West End and Enzo, having just bought an al fresco nightclub in Cefalu where he lived and where we were staying, wanted Patrick to give him some tips. I didn't know if Patrick did ever run a club, let alone one in London's West End but my doubts were allayed somewhat when we went to see the club and Patrick told Enzo that they used to smother the dance floor with salt before all the punters came so that when they started dancing the salt would get crunched up and dissolve with it rising in the air in order to make the punters thirsty so that they would drink more. Sounds feasible.

Having spent ten wonderful days in Cefalu and having met a beautiful 16 year old Italian girl by the name of, of course Maria, who I later went to visit in Milan where she lived, we made our way back home, going straight up the middle of Italy to the most beautiful city of Florence and then turning left to a place called Roquebrune just over the border of Italy into France that looked down on Monte Carlo where Patricks mum and dad, who had retired from being the chief wine waiter of the Moulin Rouge in Paris for 25 years lived, where we stayed for a couple of nights before we made our way back up to Paris.

Many years later, I entered a competition on Radio London, whereby the prize was to fly to Monaco to see Glenn Hoddle play against Paris St. Germain after he'd been transferred from Spurs. The question was, 'Which club did Hoddle score his first league goal against?' I knew the answer was Stoke City and called into the show as quick as I could. Someone from the radio station answered my call and asked me for the answer which I gave correctly. The guy said "Great, now the only problem is, the caller before you won as he gave the correct answer but we need your details as back up should he, for whatever reason, not be able to go." I thought talk about the Lord giveth in one hand and taketh away in the other. I never heard back from the station but I was determined to go and there was an advert in the then 'Shoot' football magazine advertising a two night stay to go to Monte Carlo to see Glen play in the game, I think it was for £199, obviously £398 what with my wife going as well. I phoned my friend Tony at Air France and told him what had happened with regards to the competition and the ad in the magazine, to which he responded to by saying he could get me two flight tickets at a ridiculously low price and then all I had to do was to contact Patrick Grillo at Air France in Paris to see if my wife and I could stay with his parents, which I did. Patrick said it would be fine, in fact he said he'd come with us and meet us at Nice Airport as it was over Easter. We arrived in Nice on the Friday where we met up with Patrick and went up to Roquebrune to meet his parents, my wife for the first time but me once again, as I'd already met them on the trip back from Sicily a couple of years earlier. Somehow, one of Patrick's uncles arranged to get us three free tickets for the game that was to be played the next day Saturday in the evening, as he was quite well known in the principality being a 'Marshal' for the Monaco Grand Prix and knowing people in the Monaco Football club. Patrick had to collect the tickets on the Saturday afternoon on the day of the game at the ground and took my wife and I with him but on the way, we called into a fruit and veg market where his two uncles, one of which who got us the tickets, worked and had stalls as market traders. It was around noon when the market closed and we met up with his uncles and their market trading friends in a bar in the corner of the market. There were about twelve of them, all drinking Pastis and we were invited to join them. I didn't like the taste of aniseed balls, which is what Pastis tastes of, when I was a kid but 'When in Rome.' After a couple, I thought it only right that I should pay my way and buy them all a drink, fearing that it, being in Monte Carlo, would cost me 'an arm and a leg' but alas no, the round only came to about £14 in sterling. I think the thing was that, although Monte Carlo had a reputation of being for the rich and wealthy, the likes of postman and refuge collectors had to drink somewhere and if you knew where they were, or looked hard enough, you'd find bars that accommodated the workers of the principality such as the bar in the corner of the market.

After a while, longer than we intended, we said goodbye to his uncles and went down to Monaco's ground where my wife and I waited on the concourse outside the main entrance whilst Patrick went in to get the tickets, them as they turned out not being any old tickets, they were 'Billets d'Honneur' with us sitting only a little distance from Prince Albert.

We were standing on the concourse in the blazing hot sun, when my wife started digging me in the ribs saying "Look who's over there!"

As I looked to my left, there he was in all his glory, sporting a white shell suit, white trainers, Ray Bans and a mullet, Glenn himself.

At this time, my wife and I had a Uni-Sex boutique that we named 'Sloppy Joe's' in Loughton High Road at the foot of Trapps Hill, that was often visited by what would now be known as 'A-Listers,' Such as Bobby Moore's wife Tina and her daughter Roberto and Roberto's friend Terry Venables's daughter, Sean Brooks, the Leyton Orient player who lived above the shop in a flat whose dad Johnny played for Spurs in the '50s and even Rod Stewart who was living nearby in Epping, albeit Rod didn't quite make it in, he was chased away to his Rolls Royce by some screaming girls just when he was to walk in the door, shame really, I could have reminded him of that story I told earlier in the book when he, after ordering a load of drinks when he was playing football for Highgate Redwing didn't have the money to pay for them. My wife and I were in our 40s when we had the boutique and we really enjoyed the lifestyle that emanated from having it, such as being wined and dined by the clothes manufacturers In-Wear & Martinique whose clothes we sold and ordered on a boat on a trip in the evening on The Thames modelled by some beautiful models. We also had a most beautiful young lady who used to work for us in the shop, Lyndsey, who got us invited to many parties along with her young friends, her dad being an east end bookmaker who let us use his apartment in Aloha Golf in

Puerto Banus all free I might add, that we were so grateful of. One of my only regrets that I have in life other than not actually living in Spain, happened in the Aloha Golf vicinity in Nueva Andalucia in a bar that was there by the name of El Jardin, a very popular bar with ex-pats that lived in the area and those that had holiday homes there. Ledley King, the ex-Spurs player and in my eyes the best centre back that England never had because of his injuries, had his own bar stool in there so he could sit at the end of the bar when he was on holiday but one afternoon my wife and I were walking out of it having had a quick drink on the way back to our apartment, when I noticed Simon Jordan the one-time Crystal Palace Chairman sitting on his own on the veranda drinking, with his long blonde hair and looking all very tanned. As we walked by him, he looked up and our eyes sort of met and we both nodded. I don't know why to this day I never stopped to speak to him, there was no-one else around it being mid-afternoon and scorching hot, with most people being down the beach or around their pool. I always thought he'd be a very interesting person to talk to which has been proved listening to him on Talksport as he does now,

It was a pity, we really enjoyed having the boutique but unfortunately, the 15% interest rate in the late 80s came along, which was only for a relatively short time but long enough for it to crucify us, making us having no option but to sell it.

Anyway back to Glenn and Monaco, I thought I'd never have another opportunity to speak to him, so we went up to him and introduced ourselves mentioning that we both knew his school friend who had a shop a few doors away from ours by the name of Tracey Wilkes, which drew a complete blank. So I asked him if he was waiting for his family to arrive or something, just to break the ice to which he responded by saying "No, we've just finished a team meeting." I replied "You haven't been dropped have you, only we've come all the way to see you play tonight?" To which he replied in a very arrogant way I'm afraid to say, "What me? Uh!" As if to say 'you must be joking. He seems to have grown up and mellowed over the years but I must say, he never came across that friendly, in fact my wife pulled me away and said "Come on let's go, he obviously isn't interested in speaking to us."

My Air France friend Tony, left the company and took early retirement to emigrate to South Africa where he got married.

A leaving party was organised for him, not at Air France's offices but close by in the restaurant of Air New Zealand where his friend Lee worked, who has since joined him over in South Africa.

I was asked to say something about Tony at the party but it came as a surprise, I had nothing prepared or rehearsed and I was a bit apprehensive in getting up in front of all of his work colleagues to speak to but I knew I couldn't refuse. I was somewhat lucky, as I'd recalled a story about Tony's dad that always got a laugh when I told it. His dad was a brilliant trumpet player and played in jazz bands and he also loved a bet. Unfortunately, whilst in his local betting shop in Ponders End in east Enfield where they lived, his dad, having just collected £100 in winnings sadly collapsed and had a heart attack and died, being excited by the amount he won I presume.

Anyway, during the 2nd World War, a siren sounded to let everyone know that there was an air raid starting to happen. Tony's dad grabbed Tony's mum by the hand and proceeded to drag her out of the back of the house along the garden path to an Anderson shelter situated at the bottom of the garden for them to take cover in. Tony's mum slipped her hand from his dad's grasp to run back into the house. Tony's dad shouted "Where are you going?" She replied "I haven't got my false teeth in." To which he replied "You silly cow, they're dropping fucking bombs not ham sandwiches." Which did get a laugh even though I used the 'F' word that I thought wouldn't have been welcomed. Tony's kept onto my wife and I to go and visit him since he went but I don't see any pleasure in flying in a plane to Johannesburg for twelve hours only to be shot at when I got off of it, an experience Tony's friend Lee has experienced on a couple of occasions since he's been there.

The 70s generally, was a depressing time if you were a Spurs fan. Firstly in '71, we had to endure the indignity of seeing Arsenal win the double on our own White Hart Lane pitch, although we did have a bit of a revenge when we beat Wolves in an F.A. Cup semi-final replay at Arsenal's Highbury ground to enable us to go on to win the final in 1981. We also won the EUFA Cup in 1972 but then things really went downhill with the terrible scenes in Rotterdam in '74, when our fans rioted which made Billy Nick personally speak into the P.A. to try and get the fans to restore some kind of order.

I think that did it for Bill, he being a big disciplinarian and all that. I remember him having a go at Steve Perryman once in the White Hart Lane car park when he was late for training, I was parking my B.T. van to remedy a fault on Tottenham's phone system. Bill said to him "Perryman you're late," to which Steve replied "Yeah, but only five minutes" to which Bill replied "You're still late."

Bill not long after resigned, with most of the senior players i.e. Knowles, England, Chivers & Peters going at pretty much the same time.

I was going to go to Rotterdam to see us play Feyenoord but for some reason that I can't now remember, I called off at the last minute as it turned out luckily, albeit I did go to Holland shortly after.

As said earlier, I did turn out for the College of All Saints at football but also for their volleyball team, another sport that I really enjoyed playing. We had a game against what was then called

Walthamstow Technical College, which later changed it's name to North East London Polytechnic. Incidentally, Walthamstow Technical College was a great venue to see rock bands. Back in the late 60s and 70s. I remember seeing The Stones there and Vinegar Joe, the band made up of amongst others Robert Palmer and in the day, the beautiful Elkie Brooks, who was never adverse in showing her thigh right up to her knickers by virtue of a slit right up the side of a full length dress that she wore.

Back to the volleyball match. As we were about to start, I noticed this beautiful blonde girl on the other side of the net playing for them and I thought to myself "I'm having some of that" which I did. Onika was her name who was quite a girl, she once ran naked, except with a large Fedora type hat on through a bar of the Cranbrook pub in Ilford much to everyone's joy and amazement. She was really good at volleyball, so much so that afterwards it transpired that she had played for the Swedish national volleyball team. We started a relationship and went out together for about three months, when all of a sudden she suffered a problem with her cartilage. She'd previously suffered with a similar problem in her other knee, so the Swedish Volleyball Association decided to fly her back to her native country to have them removed or whatever you have done with them. She asked me if I'd like to go out there and visit her whilst she recuperated which I duly accepted. I took two weeks off of my annual leave, as at the time I was working with B.T.

It was only into about three days of me going there when this ex-boyfriend appeared on the scene and off they went out together for a day, leaving me in the house in Vanamo, a town with a population of 600 where she lived with her non-speaking English mum & dad, who were really nice people actually. The only blessing at the time, was that Sweden were playing Italy in the Davis Cup at tennis with Bjorn Borg being the star player for Sweden, which I could watch on TV. I got so angry and stressed that I decided I'd cut my visit short and come back to England but there wasn't a travel agents I could get to, so I had to make her mum & dad understand that I wanted to phone my friend Tony at Air France in London to alter my SAS (Scandinavian Air Services) flight back to London, which I was able to do for the next day.

When Onika returned in the evening, I told her what I'd done only for her to be all regretful and sorry begging me to stay but I said "No the damage had been done." She knew that I could have done what I did with regards to changing my air ticket, as I'd taken her and her younger sister who came over to visit her in London up to Air France to meet Tony a few weeks before. Luckily, her and her mum & dad drove me the hour and a half's journey the next day to Gothenburg for me to catch my flight, so that was that the end of a fine romance.

When I returned to England, I decided that rather than waste the nine days left of my annual leave I'd return to work if I could and have the days off later but my what they called, 'line manager,' got awkward and refused. We never did get on, his name was Alf Rawlinson, a bald tall upright ex-military man and me with my long dark hair. In fact once, I tore my ankle ligaments playing football over a weekend and rang in to work Monday morning to say that I couldn't go in. I reckon it was because he didn't believe me, as about an hour later he came round to where I lived with an excuse to get my B.T. van keys so that someone else could drive it. This was when I was living in Baronet Road in Tottenham with my parents, sharing a house with a couple downstairs, with only one door between us to gain entrance. There were two door bells, one for each of us but my line manager pressed the wrong one and got the chap downstairs instead of me upstairs. Now this is where it all turned into a 'Monty Python' type sketch. The chap downstairs was named Alf and my dad's name was Alf, so when 'downstairs Alf answered the door 'Alf Rawlinson' the caller said, "Is Mr. Ray in?" Now 'downstairs Alf' thinking that he meant my dad, shouted up the stairs "Alf!" I shouted down from my bedroom where I was laid up, "Who is it Alf?" So 'downstairs Alf asked the caller "Who are you?" To which he replied "It's Alf." With 'downstairs Alf' shouting back up again "It's Alf" So, I hobbled downstairs in my pyjama bottoms making sure he could see my severely bandaged ankle so that he could go away with his tail between his legs.

Luckily my friend Billy, had heard about a guy who was buying left hand drive Volkswagen mini-buses from Aussies that had driven them across Europe but didn't have any use for them once they'd got to Holland because of the steering wheel being on the other side. Unfortunately for him, the guy had got greedy in shipping them over to the UK and was eventually caught by the customs authorities who put him in prison. He'd made a lot of money doing it, so Billy thought he'd have a crack at it albeit doing it a bit more sensibly, like two a month. He asked me if I fancied going with him and not having anything else to do not being able to go back to work, I said I would. We got a train to Harwich where we caught the ferry to the Hook of Holland and then a train to Amsterdam. It was a Friday, so we booked into a hotel when we arrived with the intention of meeting a guy that Billy got a phone number for the next day the Saturday who converted left hand drive vehicles to right hand. Once we got checked into the hotel we had a shower and as you do when in Amsterdam, we went out on the piss. I'd never been with a prostitute, in fact I haven't been with one since, so we walked around the 'Red Light' district out of curiosity just to see what all the fuss was about. There were some really pretty ones, most of them being from Holland I assume not like now, mostly Eastern Europeans. We came across this most beautiful girl standing around, so Billy and I had an argument as to who should go over to ask her how much she charged. I lost the toss, so I approached her and said all coyly, as don't forget we were only in our mid twenties "Are you working and if so how much do you charge?" She replied "Yes and it's 40 guilder (as it was then) half naked and 80 guilder fully naked" which I thanked her for. I went back to Billy who was standing with his back to a canal, who asked me like a little excited kid "What did she say, what did she say?" I said 40 guilder half naked and 80 guilder fully naked." To which he replied "Which half's naked?" I said "Oh fuck, I didn't ask her that." So we walked off and went on the as I said previously piss.

The next day a Saturday, we booked out of our hotel in the morning and set off to find the guy who had the garage converting the right hand buses to left hand. We found him in his garage which was situated under a town house in a mews in a really nice part of Amsterdam. He obviously knew what he was dong as he was working on a Volkswagen Beetle that had a miniature Rolls Royce bonnet on it with the Rolls emblem on the front.

Billy had a chat with him and bought a left hand drive bus that he had in the workshop that he'd just converted. We then went to the Amsterdam Central Station to see if we could book a ferry passage back to England, only to be told that because it was in the middle of summer they were all fully booked for about three weeks. 'They' suggested the only hope we'd have of getting a passage back to England quicker, was to go to The Hook of Holland to see if there would be a cancellation. One of the things we decided we wanted to do whilst in the city, was to go to Vondelpark which at the time, was the place to go where the hippies hung out and 'smoked' to their hearts content. We decided to go there before we made the journey home and came out of the station to go around the large square that was in front of it. We got stuck at some traffic lights, in, in effect, a two lane situation. When the lights changed, a girl that was on a bike by the kerb on the inner lane went to push off but she somehow lost her balance and came into the path of a car which in turn came over to our lane and collided with us, we being unable move to avoid the car as we were next to a tram. Billy and the guy in the other car pulled over to assess the damage, with the guy in the car ranting at us in Dutch, which is what he thought we were, as we still had Dutch number plates on our vehicle, saying that it was our fault. I said to Billy just give him your insurance details and let the insurance company sort it out. To my astonishment Billy said, "There's only one problem with that John, I don't have any." I said to him "You're fucking joking," but alas not, the guy in the car in broken English then demanded to see our passports as he said he had the right to do, as he was a customs officer. We told him that they were back at the hotel, so he said he would follow us back there to see them. The only problem was, they were in the back of the bus as we'd booked out of the hotel in the morning. Anyway, we set off and decided to take him to where we bought the bus in the hope that the guy who we bought it off of could repair his damage and we'd pay him for it. When we got there, we rang his bell but it being now Saturday afternoon, he wasn't anywhere to be seen, probably having only worked in the morning. The guy in the car said in broken English, "This no hotel, this no hotel", to which we replied "No, but this is where we're staying so it's a sort of hotel." With that he said to his wife, who was sitting in the car with his two daughters, "You wait here, I'm going to call the police," as remember, this was pre-mobile days, so off he went round the corner to find a phone box. Billy and I just looked at each other and being of the same thought, jumped in the bus and proceeded to drive off only for the guy's wife to put her hand on the car horn to draw her husband's attention. As we went round the corner, he was running back and we nearly ran him over.

We drove around Amsterdam's narrow streets and over bridges to get away only to find ourselves stuck in a cul-de-sac, it was like being in the BBC drama series Van Der Valk. We got our bags and ran off to a pedestrianized area to find a phone box so that Billy could phone his girlfriend to contact his insurance broker to get his insurance backdated to the time he bought the vehicle. We went into a few bars to give her time to sort it out, then called her back a couple of hours later. Fortunately, she got the insurance sorted so we made our way back to the bus, skirting around it in case the police were waiting for us to return but fortunately there was no sign of any, so we jumped into the bus and made our way down to the Hook of Holland. When we arrived, we only had to wait for a short while before we got a cancellation back to England. That in the end was the easy part, the problem I could foresee was that the police may had notified the border controls of the incident in Amsterdam but also, that I had TOTTENHAM as my place of birth on my passport and I was cacking myself that the passport controller checking my passport, was a Feyenoord fan and may have taken out retribution on me for the Tottenham fans behaviour in the football match a little while earlier but luckily neither happened as it turned out.

As I said earlier, the mid 70s was a depressing time to be a Spurs fan, what with all the better players coming to the end of their careers and Billy Nick leaving the club. The board in their infinite wisdom, chose to replace Bill with a 'dyed-in-the-wool' Arsenal man Terry Neil, what were they thinking? Our crowd of friends used to stand in the lower West Stand Enclosure around this time to watch the games, right under the directors box where once David Cassidy was seen seated, in his full length fur coat. There was so much anger and abuse directed at the directors when they made the decision to appoint Terry Neil, so much so, it made a guy that stood with us, Harry was his name, whose parents had Mark Bowen the ex-Spurs player staying in 'digs' with them, haul himself up on the wooden surround that encompassed the directors box, the same surround incidentally that Jayne Mansfield, the American blonde beautiful actress was seen sitting on the edge of in a photograph taken half-time during a game v Wolves in the 50s, to spit his chewing gum at him as he walked down the steps to take his front row seat.

Just to say, with regards to the above, there was a rumour that Jayne Mansfiedl had the hots for the Spurs centre-forward at the time Bobby Smith, similarly Danny Blanchflower supposedly had a fling with Alma Cogan the 50s/60s singer who resided in Highgate, so that's Danny Blanchflower and John Lennon that Alma Cogan had an affair with then, 'allegedly' as they say, don't know if either are true but they sound good.

The Enclosure, was a great place to stand, as it was within hearing distance of the players and officials so you could hurl any abuse that you wanted to for them to pick up.

I remember Air France Tony once shouting at a linesman, who'd missed an 'obvious' off-side decision against Spurs "Oi, linesman, stick your flag up" with the aforementioned 'spitting chewing gum Harry' adding "Yeah, up your fucking arse then wave it."

That's what I loved about football was the off-field banter.

OBSERVATIONS

At this juncture relating to fans, I've got three questions if anyone knows the answers to:-

1. When a team attacks the opponents goal and shoots or heads the ball goalwards but the ball goes just over the bar or just wide, why do the fans of that team clap and cheer. I thought the idea was to put the ball into the back of the net.

2. Why do fans 'boo?' It sounds so childish. Call the ref a wanker or something but not 'boo.' In fact I've never been next to someone who's ever 'booed,' perhaps it's the broadcasters making a soundover or something.

3. Why do fans cheer when the floodlights fail? I suppose they just assume that they're automatically coming back on. I bet they wouldn't if they didn't, mind you the only time I recall that they haven't was in a West Ham v Palace game in '97.

4. Why do the commentators say "The linesman has put his 'offside' flag up." How many flags does he carry?

5. How comes there's a 'second ball?' There's only one on the pitch at any given time.

6. How can the ball hit the back of the net? Surely the back of the net is behind the goal. When a goal's scored the ball hits the front of the net.

n.b. Incidentally, when I used to coach the Norfolk County Schools teams (more of that later), I used to wind the lads up by putting balls on the edge of the area and betting them they couldn't hit 'the back of the net from there.' You should have seen their faces when they thought they had succeeded when I told them they hadn't and explained why.

Back to the banter. Some years after standing in the enclosure, I bought a season ticket for a seat in the first tier of the 'old' Paxton Road stand. It was a great view from behind the goal, right down to the other end of the Park Lane goal. I remember we played Sheffield Wednesday, with Tony Galvin & Chris Waddle in their side, David Pleat having sold Galvin to them and Waddle joining them having done a stint in Marseille who we'd sold him to.

Now to tell this story is going to include some tactical explanation so bear with. Wednesday were attacking, the ball was with Waddle who had it wide on their right on the half way line, so Tottenham's back four had to adapt to counteract the attack, pushing their left back, Hughton or Mitchell Thomas I can't recall now, up onto Waddle with the other three of the back four forming a defensive diagonal formation backwards towards our goal, with Gary Stevens our right back being the deepest of the four albeit on the right hand side. Waddle hit a superb ball across the half way line to Tony Galvin out on the left wing. Now Air France Tony was of the thought, that Chrissie Hughton the Spurs left back, was never the same player if Galvin wasn't playing in front of him as Galvin had a terrific work ethic, anyway I digress. Tony Galvin's penchant whenever he received the ball on the left wing was to run as fast as he could direct to the corner flag and would then either, attempt to cross the ball with his weaker left foot, with three out of four of the crosses going behind the goal or, when he arrived there to bring the ball back onto his stronger right foot but then, very often, leaving his attacker/s offside as the opponents defenders would be able to buy time to adjust and move up.

To adapt to, if you like this reverse situation, the back four would need to swivel around so that our left back would be the deepest defender and with Stevens our right back moving up to close down Galvin on the half way line, which encouraged someone to shout from behind me, given how I described Galvin's penchant for playing as within the previous paragraph "Stevens, don't waste your time running up to him, wait for him at the corner flag."

Another situation I remember, was when Spurs goalkeeper Erik Thorsvedt was playing albeit with a bad knee at the time and couldn't take goal kicks. Spurs had 'Gudni' Bergsson the Icelandic player playing at right back at the same time and because Erik couldn't take the goal kicks, he got Bergsson to take them. Again, someone from around where I was seated shouted out, "Look, Thorsvedt can't take the goal kick with his 'bad knee' so he's taking it with his 'Gudni.'"

Not quite a 'banter' story but in a similar vein, my friend Barry, remember him earlier with the 'This Is Your Life' marriage story? Well he had a season ticket seat where I had mine albeit some years after and he had a friend who had a seat season ticket about twelve seats along in the same row. He borrowed his friend's ticket so that he could take his young daughter and when he arrived for the game, he asked the guy next to him, who he'd got to know over a period of time, if he'd mind swapping seats so that his daughter could sit next to Barry her dad. The guy didn't mind at all but a problem arose during the game, when the guy got, to say at least, upset with a referees decision that denied Spurs a goal. To show his disgust, he tore the plastic back off his seat and threw it, 'frisby' style, down towards the referee, just missing the people in the wheelchaired enclosure down the front on the way. Of course, the stewards all converged on him but the fans around him convinced the stewards to 'lay off' so that they could deal with it themselves, which they did in no uncertain terms. The problem though was, that of course, it was my friend Barry's friend's seat officially and he probably would have been the one that got barred for life albeit it all got sorted out before that could happen.

As if things couldn't have got any worse on the pitch, around the 74-5 season they did, by virtue of the club suffering the indignity of being relegated to the 2nd Division in the 76-77 season, the last time them being there in the 49-50 season. Actually, there's a photograph of me in Stevie Perryman's autobiography on Page 154 down in the left hand corner with long hair facing the camera when there was a 'demand' from the fans for the team to appear in the directors box on the last home game of the season even though they'd been relegated. God knows why but I suppose it shows the true loyalty of the fans that have suffered the club through good and bad times. Funny thing is, it wasn't all bad, as being relegated we were able to go to grounds that we'd never been before or having a chance as it turned out, of going to in the future e.g. Notts County's Meadow Lane, Mansfield's Field Mill and Bolton's old Burnden Park before they moved into their new University of Bolton Stadium which some will argue, has caused their financial demise of late.

Fortunately, we only lasted one season in the 2nd Division gaining promotion in 77-78. During the close season at the end of it, myself Chris (Rotters), his friend Barry and my friend Air France Tony played a game of tennis and went for a drink afterwards in the Green Dragon pub in Winchmore Hill in

North London. I remember us sitting round a table agreeing that we couldn't hope to survive in the 1st Division with the players that Keith Burkeishaw had at his disposal but little were we to know that within a couple of days, he would sign the two Argentinians Ossie Ardiles & Ricky Villa, In the words of Victor Meldrew

"We couldn't believe it."

The opening game of the '78-9 season was against Nottingham Forest away, with Ricky scoring on his debut. I remember it quite vividly, as I was getting married on the day to my first wife down in Bridgewater, the town that inspired Simon & Garfunkel to write their hit record 'Trouble Over Bridgewater.' I was 33 at the time with the relationship that I had with my wife prior to the wedding a comparatively long one, as apart from the relationship that I had with Gilly mentioned earlier being somewhat lengthy, I hated having to break off long term relationships with girls and I suppose having them break up with me.

The wedding itself took a lot of planning, as not only did my family travel down from London but so too did all of my close friends and football playing pals. They all travelled down on the day on a Grey-Green coach driven by my cousin Ian, who was a part-time driver for them as well as being a BT engineer as I was and a decent footballer himself. I travelled down a day earlier on the Friday, along with Air France Tony, his work colleague Johnny Waring and his wife Trish. We stopped at a pub in Yeovil where Johnny knew the publican, a guy by the name of, coincidentally, Johnny Walker, no not the D.J., Johnny Walker was in his time a very good goalkeeper having played with Johnny Waring for the likes of Croydon Amateurs and Tooting & Mitcham. I was quintessentially a 'city' boy not appreciating the countryside at all and I do remember whilst we were having lunch in the pub, some lads walking past the pub window with their rifles cocked over their shoulders having gone out shooting I imagine, it was like a scene from Susan George's film Straw Dogs. We stayed for a couple of hours and when we left , we promised the landlord that we would return there on the following Sunday the day after the wedding for lunch on our way back to London in the coach.

We arrived in Bridgewater late afternoon and booked into our hotel and in the evening, myself and Air France Tony went out with my newly to become brother-in-law and a couple of his friends, as I couldn't have a stag do as such, as all my friends were coming down the next day the day of the wedding. My soon to be brother-in-law turned out to be hilarious. He was telling us that a couple of weeks before, he'd gone out on a stag-do and that there were eight of them, the bridegroom and seven others which was convenient for the purpose of this story. They went to their preferred local pub first and ordered eight pints of Guinness, albeit knowing full well that one of them had been barred from the pub some weeks before. They waited until the publican had almost poured the eight pints before the guy who was barred came in. When the publican looked up after pouring the last pint, he recognised the fella and shouted at him that he had been barred. The others almost begged the publican to re-consider under the circumstances of 'it' being a stag-do but the publican wouldn't budge, so they all walked out with the publican left with eight pints of Guinness on his hands all unpaid for. With this, they started off on their pub crawl. As they went into the first pub they said to the bridegroom ,"You go in and order a pint for yourself and when the barman pours it and you go to drink it order seven half pints, The barman will then ask who the seven halves are for and you can then put your hands up to your mouth and shout out at the top of your vice 'Hi-ho!' and then we'll come in on our hands and knees singing 'Hi-ho, hi-ho it's off to work we go" a la the Seven Dwarfs, which wouldn't be allowed now because of the coronavirus only six being a maximum. The bridegroom agreed to do it and it worked a treat, with the packed pub full of drinkers clapping and cheering. It worked so well that the bridegroom couldn't wait to do it again at the second pub they went to and the third. When they got to the fourth pub, they did it again but this time, as was pre-planned by the seven, when the barman asked the bridegroom who the seven halves were for, he put his hands up to his mouth yelling "Hi-ho" but nothing, he did it again "Hi-ho," again nothing, as they'd all left him there high and dry and pissed off to another pub.

The 'church' wedding the next day went really well, with all my friends and family down from London with all the locals from Bridgewater not knowing what hit them and of course with Ricky Villa scoring on his debut at Forest being an added bonus.

My wife and I had been living together for a few years, so we didn't bother with a honeymoon, so we went back to London on the coach driven by my cousin, in fact, we may not even had got married, not that we didn't want to, we were quite happy just living together but we were put under pressure by my wife's father who was giving us some money to buy our first house but wouldn't if we didn't. He was a lovely man, Sav was his name, he was Italian and ended up in Bridgewater as a prisoner of war. I remember once saying to him "Sav, have you ever been to London?" To which he replied in broken English, putting an 'a' on the end of every word as Italians do, "Only the oncea but I didn'ta like ita as the machinea tooka my ticketa." It turns out he went on the underground and put his ticket in the machine to commence his journey but didn't take it out as he went through the barrier. When he got to the other end of his journey he didn't have a ticket to go through the barrier to in effect end his journey and had to go to the ticket collector to get out. The ticket collector asked him where his ticket was to which Sav replied "I don'ta knowa the machinea ita teke ita." Well why would you know what to do if you couldn't read and understand the ticket instruction signs?

As said, we travelled back to London on the Sunday via the pub that myself, Air France Tony and Johnny Waring and his wife stopped at on the way down, on the way stopping to see a penalty being taken on a local Sunday morning football park pitch. We were going along when someone on the coach shouted "Penalty." My cousin driving the coach, automatically slammed on his anchors so that we could see it being taken and consequently scored which culminated in a big cheer going up. To say that Johnny Walker the publican in the Yeovil pub was pleased to see us was an understatement. When he saw the coach he must straightaway have been thinking 'ching ching.' Actually that apart, he was pleased that we kept our promise in returning there and to some degree it put the 'icing on the cake' as far as the wedding weekend went, with my now wife enjoying it as she was there.

We got chatting to some local lads who were all footballers themselves, some playing for Yeovil Town and we discussed the possibility of returning in a few weeks to play what turned out for them to be a pre-season friendly game.

We went back there again, with my cousin driving the coach and fought out an enjoyable 3-3 draw. I think it's fair to say they were very impressed with the standard of players we had, especially with them being half of Yeovil Town and players from other clubs of a similar standard, in fact, I played left wing in the game and the right back who was up against me played for Bristol Rovers.

Things didn't turn out at all well following Ricky Villa's debut goal in the 1-1 draw away to Forest, it was all a bit of a false dawn, the following game we lost 4-1 at home to Villa then shortly after at home to Swansea 3-1 and then we got a hammering at Liverpool 7-0.

That 78-9 season was a real damp squib, the only good thing I remember about it was meeting a guy by the name of Chris

Chapman for the first time, when myself and Air France Tony went with Chris (Rotters) in his car up to Carrow Road to see us play Norwich. On the way, we picked Chris Chapman up at a roundabout just outside Harlow. We shook hands on being introduced to him by Chris(Rotters) and straightaway he said "Right, what are we playing then cricket?" I imagined him doing a bit of Origami with some paper and making a wicket a bat and rolling up some paper for a ball but alas no. He came up with this game that was pub name related, the rules being that the two in the front of the car and the two in the rear, on this occasion that being myself and Air France Tony would toss up as to who was to bat and who was to bowl. The rules were, that if you went past a pub that had a name that had 'limbs' in its title, then you would get that relevant number of runs e.g. The British Queen or The Red Lion you would get four runs for, as within the number of arms and legs they had. The only problem was though, if you were to go past a pub with say the Coach & Horses or the 'Limping Centipede' as its name, you could gain an infinite number of runs as you wouldn't know how many horses would be pulling the coach so you'd have to limit the number of runs you'd get, say 16 or something. If you went past a pub that didn't have 'limbs' within it's title e.g. The Crown, then the other team would gain a wicket. The problem is nowadays, most long journies are carried out along motorways so it's difficult to play but our journey up to Norwich could be taken by the old A11 through Mount Fitchett, Sawbridgeworth and Saffron Walden before the M11 was built, then again on the old A11 before it was re-built around Thetford. Tony and I got to near Attleborough when we'd lost our ten wickets for around 97 runs. When the two Chris's in front went into 'bat,' we arrived in Norwich and they were something like 84 for 7 but we were so engrossed in the game we carried on to nearly Yarmouth to finish it. We arrived back in Norwich just in time for the game to kick off, a game in which the Spurs keeper Aleksic caught a ring on his finger in the goal netting which nearly tore his finger off which made him have to leave the field of play only for Glenn Hoddle to replace him in goal, as he did when we beat Manchester United at Old Trafford in a League Cup game in 1980, when again Aleksic had to leave the field when he received a broken jaw following a challenge with United's Joe Jordan who later became the assistant coach to Harry Redknapp when he became manager of Tottenham. The next season, again we made the journey up to Norwich to see a game, this time six of us, three in each of two cars. On the way back, we stopped at a pub in a little village on the old A11 in Essex named Newport.

We had a few drinks and a game of darts when Chris Chapman decided we should have a game of horse racing. Similarly to the cricket, I'd never heard of it but he then requested a pack of playing cards from behind the bar. He proceeded to take the four aces out of the pack of cards and place them down, face up, at the bottom of the table which represented four horses. This left 48 cards in the park which he shuffled. He then took the first seven cards off the top of the pack of cards in turn and placed them 'up' the table again face-up from where the four aces/horses were placed so that they would represent each furlong in a seven furlong race. Now this is going to take some explaining in writing but Chris nominated himself as the banker, the idea being that he would take one card in turn off the top of the remaining pack of cards and depending on what suit each turned over card represented would determine which of the four number laid out aces/horses would progress up the table in the seven furlong race. Now to determine the odds as to what ace/horse would win, if say e.g. there were 5no. cards representing 'clubs' in the seven overturned cards that made up the furlongs, then there were less clubs of that suit in the remaining pack, so by definition the ace/horse card that represented that suit had less chance of winning, so in effect, it would be an outsider and you could lay odds of say 20-1. Alternatively if e.g. there were no 'Diamonds' in the seven laid out cards, again, by definition, there'd be more diamonds left in the park so the diamond ace/horse would have more chance of winning so that would be favourite at say odds of evens. I tell ya, the game started out as just us six playing but in the end the whole of the bar was taking part.

Chris knew more games than Waddingtons. Five of us went down to Gillingham on a Wednesday evening to see Spurs play a pre-season friendly, Chris being one of us. On the way back, he decided we'd play another game. I thought well, it can't be the cricket game as it was too dark to see the pub names. So he came up with the idea that each of us would put a fiver 'in the pot' and we'd each draw out a name of petrol stations by the name of the oil companies that they represented, with the one of us, who had drawn out the oil company of the most garages that we went past winning all of the money. Ingenious.

I must say I am a big fan of games of the aforementioned type. I remember one time, my wife and I were staying in a friend of mine's apartment in Aloha Golf up in the hills behind Marbella's Puerta Bonus, where as I mentioned previously I missed out on talking to the Crystal Palace Chairman at the time Simon Jordan. A bar we liked to frequent up there was one named 'The Links Bar,' where many of the Aloha Golf Club members used to go to socialise in after playing a round, as they preferred it to the bar in the golf club. I was standing at the bar one Sunday afternoon waiting for the early game to start on SKY which they had in there. I noticed a cellophane pocket with a sheet of names in it, so inquisitively I asked the guy behind the bar what it was. He explained that every Sunday afternoon, all the customers on the sheet would have a competition whereby they had to forecast the actual 'scores' of the two games being shown. They would put 10 Euros into it every week and because to forecast the two scores was so difficult the 'pot' could mount up quite considerably, in fact on the day, there was 1200 Euros in there waiting to be won.

When I returned back to England, I suggested in my local pub in the 'sleepy' village where I lived, that we should do it and everyone was keen although the ten that were in it were reluctant to put the equivalent of 10 Euros in so we settled on £1 a week. That said 'the pot' soon built up, I've won over a hundred quid a couple of times in the five or so years we've been doing it.

Another football related pub game I like which we also do, is at say15minutes from the end of a televised game, we all put two pounds in an ash tray and every time the ball goes out of play or the games stopped for a foul or goal, the ash tray with the money is passed around in a circle, until the final whistle blows and whoever is holding the money filled ash tray wins it.

There you go, some ideas for you.

Around the start of the 80-81 season when Tottenham's fortunes started to change, my second wife and I, yes my first marriage didn't last that long, started drinking in The Bull public house in Silver Street in Edmonton. At this time, we were living in Tottenham Lane in Crouch End in a top floor flat above a shop. It wasn't particularly nice but it served a purpose at the time. What we did have when we lived there this being around 1980, was a wonderful but extremely sad view of Alexandra Palace on fire . It was just like watching a movie except unfortunately you couldn't switch it off. After a short while we moved around the corner into another flat above a parade of shops right by the gates leading up to Alexandra Palace. The flat, was above a launderette that kept our flat very warm during the winter and next door to a Greek restaurant where you could take your own wine and The Victoria Stakes pub which was also very convenient. Every morning I used to have to drive over Alexandra Palace to go to Enfield to where my BT van was kept. Although the Palace itself was in a bit of a mess, the view from it looking over the city of London in one direction and Tottenham's White Hart Lane was very inspirational and would set me up for the day.

The first night I went in to The Bull, Ronnie Akers the publican, who had a remarkable resemblance to Bud Abbott, one half of the American comedy duo Abbott & Costello, welcomed me with "I hope you've washed your hands lately." Why, I couldn't understand at the time, I thought he saw me flicking a beer mat up and catching it or something but no, on the Easter Monday a couple of days previously, I was walking out of the West Stand at White Hart Lane with my wife after we'd beaten the Arsenal and I was surrounded by it seems hoards of blokes in Burberry macs all dressed the same. It was really weird but when I looked at the guy next to me, I noticed it was Dino Zoff the great Juventus goalkeeper and with the other guys all being dressed in the same macs being the Juventus team who were to play the Arsenal on the following Wednesday in the European Cup and they'd obviously all gone along to 'run the rule' over them. I couldn't resist myself, I put my hand out to him and wished him all the best on the Wednesday and he shook it saying "Grazzi." By all accounts, Ronnie was walking quite close to us and saw what happened, hence him asking me the question about washing my hands. He was a great guy was Ronnie and I spent many an hour in his pub after that, especially on the night of the FA Cup replay when we beat Man City with Ricky Villa's wonder goal, we drank into the early hours of the next day.

My BT friend Barry, the one I played tennis with when we went on that seven hour round trip to get knocked out of a tennis tournament in 25mins. had our lunch in their most days. I loved the food as Rene, Ronnie's wife, used to make tripe and brawn. We'd get in there at noon and one day, there was guy a standing at the bar with his back to it sort of 'holding court,' with about half a dozen men sitting down in front of him in a semi-circle. When I looked closer it was the comedian Frank Carson. Evidently Frank had been appearing a couple of evenings in the Starlight Rooms which was a club/entertainment venue at Enfield Town Football Club approximately 5 miles down the

A10. He was telling a story about when he was appearing on the Isle Of Man and an Irish fella, who had got into a drunken state, ended up in a police cell for a night. The police released him the next morning and asked him where he lived. He replied, he didn't live on the island he was just visiting and was staying in the 'R Ten' Hotel. The island being relatively small and the police knowing all of it, said that there was no such hotel on the island but the Irishman was adamant, he insisted that he was staying at the 'R Ten.' The police decided that they would drive him around so that he could show them where he meant. As they were driving along, the Irishman yelled out "There it is the 'R Ten Hotel' with a copper replying "You fucking idiot, that's not the 'R Ten' that's the 'RIO' Hotel as in the name of Rio de Janeiro. Actually the story sounded better in Frank's Irish brogue and just to think people had been paying to see him at the Starlight Rooms and we were getting a free show.

The Bull pub was in Edmonton's Silver Street, one end being where it met the A406 where the North Middlesex Hospital was and at the other end of Silver Street was a 'mental' hospital by the name of St. David's. Tony, one of the brothers who tried to get me to join them at Charringtons and who played for Highgate Redwing with Rod Stewart and Brian Ellerbeck, 'Eller' who sold the peanuts round the perimeter of the White Hart Lane pitch on match days and who as I wrote earlier had the confrontation with the comedian Mike Read, at the time were playing for a team named Braintree, who were up the top of the Tottenham Sunday League. One Sunday, they had a top of the league clash with a team who used the football pitch within the St. David's Hospital grounds as their home pitch. I don't know how come as, as I said, It was the Tottenham Sunday League but the hospital was in Edmonton the next in effect borough along. Braintree were losing 1-0 with a few minutes to go and were desperately trying to get an equaliser at least. There was one of the hospital patients standing about 10 yards or so from the touchline with his arms folded swaying from side to side with his feet in a position what I can only describe as a 10 to 2 situation of a clock face. The ball went out of play and landed right between the patient's feet. 'Eller' got to the touchline to take the throw in and shouted at the lad "The ball" but there was no reaction from the lad who had it between his feet and still swaying from side to side. Again 'Eller' shouted louder this time "Give me the ball" still no reaction, so this time 'Eller' ran towards him shouting at the same time "Give me the fucking ball." The lad without even looking down just kicked it even further away from the pitch some 30 yards by now with Eller running after it which caused someone to ask the question "Who should be in the hospital Eller, you or him?"

Most people in the Bull pub had a nickname, there was amongst others 'Secret Squirrel' a friend of mine's dad who was a Private Detective, 'Two Pint Pete' named so because he always had two pints in his hands and 'Vodka John,' he was one of those guys that if he liked you you were ok with him but if he didn't, then look out. Luckily he liked me so I was ok but he 'liked' my wife even more, as I since found out in later years from her that he asked her to run off with him to his parents villa in Greece.

I organised a team from the pub to enter into a sports quiz that was running at the time organised by the Sunday People. In the first round we were drawn at home to 'The London Branch of the Plymouth Argyle Supporters Club.' A couple of days before they were due to visit us, Ronnie our publican, got a call from them saying, "We may have in our team a high profile member and we thought you should be made aware, as we didn't want to turn up with him and it causing some sort of stir." It turned out that the member was going to be Michael Foot, the leader at the time of the Labour Party and a massive Argyle fan but unfortunately, because of other commitments, he never did show, which was a shame. I remember it was the first time I ever heard the chant "I can't read and I can't write but I can drive a tractor, I drive to the left and drive it to the right that's how I drive me tractor" as goaded by Vodka John towards the Argyle fans during the quiz with their Devonshire roots. We didn.t last long in the 'national' competition as we got knocked out in the next round by a team that came out of a pub opposite The Whitehall Theatre in London where Brian Rix would perform his comedy farces, most of them with his trousers round his ankles, the theatre incidentally being close to the Prime Minister's residence.

In 1982 when Tottenham played Barcelona in the European Cup-Winners Cup, we drew a 1st leg home game 1-1 when a blunder from Ray Clemence let them in for their equaliser. Vodka John and his brother, who some of you may have seen as the guy who got into the Royal Box to kiss and hug Stevie Perryman when he held the FA Cup aloft in 1981, had found out that there was availability to go out to Barcelona for the 2nd leg through a travel agent in Knightsbridge. So on the Monday before the Wednesday game, 'Vodka John,' his brother me and my wife went up there together to book tickets to go. The problem with me was, was that my friend, Air France Tony, was aware of a possible cancellation of a booking of a different trip going out there through Air France, as they were in partnership at the time with Tottenham Hotspur Travel which was associated with the club. The trip that 'Vodka John' and his brother were going on cost about £300, which included a one night stopover which was a considerable amount of money for me, whereas Air France's trip, was a 'fly-in fly-out one day trip' for £99 which suited me better. 'Vodka John' was desperate for me to join him and his brother but I decided to wait and see what happened with the other option which, as it turned out, did happen. I took the details of 'Vodka John's' hotel where he was going to stay in Barcelona whilst we were in the travel agents in anticipation, that if I did go I'd meet him there, which I told him I would at 3 o'clock in the afternoon.

On the day of the game, we arrived at Barcelona Airport around noon and were driven into the city centre by coach. We arrived at a roundabout with the coach driver through an interpreter pointing to a bar across the way saying to the fans that the coach would pick them up there at 6 p.m to go to the game. I needed to find out where the hotel was where I was to meet 'Vodka John' and his brother and asked the driver but he didn't know but at the same time a taxi pulled up right in front of the coach to let someone out of it, so I jumped off the coach and got into the taxi asking the driver to take me to the hotel, the name of which I had on a piece of paper. Straightway as I got into the taxi, it came to me, 'fuck it,' how am I going to know where to meet the coach after the game to get back to the airport?

I walked into the hotel bar as I promised I would dead on 3 o'clock and was greeted with a big cheer with 'Vodka John' shouting "Here he is." He and his brother and the rest of their entourage that had flown over for the two day trip, were as they say, already 'on the sauce.' Amongst them were three guys dressed up as angels, similar to the ones that were famous for walking around the White Hart Lane pitch on those great European Cup nights of the early 60s, albeit I should imagine, not the same people as they would have been long gone. I was quite impressed as to how Vodka John and his brother were dressed in black trousers and white shirts albeit that was all to change, as at about 6 o'clock, someone reminded everyone that the coach that was to take them to the Nou Camp would be arriving at 6.30. Vodka John and his brother disappeared for about 20 minutes, then reappeared as if they were going off to war, in jeans, a Spurs yellow away team shirt and a similar coloured bandana tied behind their heads. I just jumped onto the coach with them still not knowing how I was going to get back to the airport after the game but as I was walking along the aisle of the coach, who did I see sitting in a seat, none other than the wonderful Sunday Times and World Soccer magazine football journalist Brian

Glanville, the World Soccer magazine which I subscribed to regularly just to read his articles. I asked him if he minded me sitting next to him, to which he replied "You certainly can son." It was daylight as we travelled through the streets of Barcelona to the Nou Camp but I don't remember seeing anything of the city, as I was too engrossed in what Brian had to tell me. What a knowledgeable football man he is.

As we arrived at the stadium, the first people fortunately I set eyes on were some of those that were on the coach that took me from the airport to the city earlier in the day, so I decided to 'tug' onto them rather than hang around with Vodka John and his brother so that I could find the coach to get me back to the airport straight after the game. I went up to the seats where they were seated so that I knew where they were before going back down to the bar to get a baguette and a pint of beer. All the Spurs fans were allocated seats high up in the top tier of the stadium but I decided I would take my beer and baguette even higher up, right up to the highest row of seats and sat there with my legs dangling over the seat in front of me all alone taking in the enormity of the stadium and to eat my baguette and swig my beer. Once I finished eating, I took my beer and went onto the narrow concourse behind where I was seated to look over the wall to the view of the harbour which was made even more spectacular by the sun setting. As I was leaning on the wall, two policeman approached me and asked me to take my seat but before I did, for some reason I suppose just to be friendly, I pointed to the view and said to them in my immaculate Spanish "El vista esta bella eh?" One of the policeman must have thought I could speak fluent Spanish and started to speak to me in conversational Spanish, to which I had no idea of what he was saying, I just nodded my head and kept smiling. I went back to the seat right at the back of the stadium to watch the game until the Danish one time Charlton player and Robin Williams lookalike Allan Simonsen opened the scoring for Barcelona. I thought I needed to get into the action more and cheer the lads on, so I left my seat and went down to where all the Spurs fans were congregated lower down in the tier. I hadn't been down there long when the lights failed for a short while. During it, the Barcelona fans in the tier below us started to throw all sorts of things up at us, coins and beer cans etc. Something hit a lad who was sitting in the front row of the tier where we were, so he got up and started remonstrating with them only for the police, who were guarding us to start wading in with their batons and start whacking him. His girlfriend who was next to him, sat on his lap to prevent the police from hitting him but all they did was hit her as well. There were many of what you would call middle age responsibly minded Spurs men amongst the fans and when they saw the girl being hit, they decided 'enough was enough' and got between the girl and the police which made them back off. I thought I'd had enough of this and retreated back to my seat at the top of the stadium and I as arrived at the top of the steps there were two policemen standing there, one of which was the one that I'd had the conversation with of how beautiful the harbour view was earlier. In my anger as to what I'd just seen, I put my finger to my temple at the same time saying " Los Espanoles son loco." I then sat down when I felt a whack on my shoulder which the other policeman had given me with his baton, not the one who I'd had the conversation with earlier. As I turned round holding my shoulder, I witnessed the policeman that I'd had the conversation with pushing the other one who hit me saying something like "What are you hitting him for, he hasn't done anything."

I only went to one other away game to see Spurs play in Europe, that was in 1985 v Real Madrid. We were 1-0 down from the 1st leg and needed to claw it back in the 2nd leg in the Bernabeau Stadium. I went on this two day trip on my own, staying in a hotel on the night before the game. Around midday I decided I'd go for a walk and explore the city of Madrid. I set off pretty much aimlessly, as I didn't know the city at all well. I was walking along listening to my all time favourite album, Steve Winwood's 'Arc Of A Diver' on my Walkman, remember them? I was listening to the track coincidentally entitled 'Spanish Dancer,' when I heard a shout of "Johnny Ray." At first I thought it was coming through my headphones but when I looked around, I saw my friend Barry Williams who as I said earlier in the book, introduced me to Nigel of Dexy's Midnight Runners beckoning me into a taxi that he was in with his friends halted at some traffic lights. I ran over and jumped in and asked them where they were going to which Barry replied ,"We've got a table booked in a restaurant in the Plaza Mayor," It was a great afternoon eating and drinking in one of the most beautiful 'squares' in the world. Mind you Barry, whose best friend was and still is Chris's (Rotters.) was no stranger to extended lunch times, something he and his friends who we were with, were used to doing similarly in the City of London where they worked. Barry and his friends, were staying in the Hotel Miguel Angel while they were there, the same hotel incidentally that the Tottenham players were staying in but me, I was staying in a far less 'star numbered' hotel which I left for around 5p.m. so that I didn't incur the same experience of not knowing where my coach would be to be picked up from to go to the airport as I did when I went to Barcelona.

When I got back to the hotel, the first thing I noticed were the toilet rolls hanging out of every window of a room that a Spurs fan was occupying, it was quite a sight, the toilet rolls looking like streamers as in the 1978 World Cup in Argentina when the hosts were playing. I even had trouble trying to convince the armed policemen on the door that I was booked in there but they did let me in eventually.

When we got to the Bernabeu, Real's stadium, the first thing that impressed me was the brightness of the floodlights, they made it seem even brighter than daylight. If I remember, it was a pretty dour game, having lost the 1st leg through a Steve Perryman own goal and apart from a few attempts we didn't really look like scoring, so I came away a bit non-plussed really, we not deserving to go through.

When I left the stadium to go to where the coaches were parked, I noticed some what they call abroad 'Ultras,' yobs basically that were looking for trouble. They were making their way to where our coaches were parked, so I ran as fast as I could thinking that when I get there I'm not going to get on coach 3, which was the coach that I arrived on, I thought I'd jump on coach 1 in the hope I could avoid any ensuing trouble. As I got on the coach 1 it was quite full but I got a seat and I shouted to everyone that they should pull down the blinds so that they were tight to prevent any glass coming into the coach if the windows got smashed, as they were unaware of the pursuing 'Ultras.' Luckily, we drove off within minutes of me getting on the coach but when we arrived at the airport, some of the fans in the coaches behind us came in to the departure lounge in a right mess, many of them with serious 'cut' injuries, there was blood everywhere having been attacked by the aforementioned 'Ultras' back at the stadium.

Many of the injured didn't want to wait to get treated as the planes were about to leave, so they just suffered until they got back to Stanstead. On the way back, I sat next to a guy and we got chatting for pretty much the whole journey, I'm telling you this because his presence would be relevant to a story to be told later. I think in a way, this experience stopped me going to any more away games, as I haven't seen Spurs play away in Europe since then.

Around this time, there were a number of lads that drank in the Bull pub that played in an Edmonton Sunday morning league team by the name of Arnos. Anything that happened with regards to the administration of running the club was carried out in the pub by the club secretary who drank in there. They couldn't get anyone to run/manage the team, so the secretary, knowing I'd played at a comparatively higher level than Sunday league football and knowing that my energetic playing days were over, being on the wrong side of 40, asked me if I'd be interested in doing it. I couldn't let them down really, so I said I would. The club was never run on success, it existed on the social side of things something that all clubs on a similar level should be run on. That said, it was run very well and every 'close-season' in the summer they would organise what they'd call a 'pre-season' tour but it was just an excuse for a 'piss up' really. It was at the end of the season when they asked me to take on 'managing' the team but they'd already organised a trip to Ibiza, which I looked forward to going on albeit with a bit of trepidation as I'd not long got married to my 2nd wife. About a week or so before we were due to fly off, the whole team got invited round to one of the players house for a party. As is the norm with parties, the men were on one side of the room and the women on the other. My wife always found mens' company more exciting than womens but she did stand with them just to be sociable. On the way home she said to me, the women were trying to make her welcome in the conversations and when my wife asked did they not mind their husbands all going away together they replied "No we trust them" to which my wife replied "Yeah right." I think it was a case of as they say 'What happens on tour stays on tour.'

It was a five day trip and we stayed in San Antonio, in fact we had a game arranged against the San Antonio local team. Of course, most of the lads couldn't wait to get out on the town as soon as we got there but myself and another couple of the 'mature' lads didn't go straight to a bar that the others had virtually taken over, we went into a bar across from the hotel where there was a guy playing jazz on a piano and where we could play backgammon whilst listening to him, before joining the rest of the lads at the aforementioned bar they'd taken over later on.

We got there about 1a.m. and it was jumping and packed with all our crowd in there virtually as said taking the place over. Myself and the other two guys I was with went to the bar to get a drink where we were crammed up against three blondes in high heels, black leather mini-skirts and jackets to match. They said they came from Warrington, a town in the north west of England that always had a good name for attractive blonde ladies for some reason, I found out that they came from there as I said to one of the girls, "Where do you come from?" She replied "Warrington." So I said, "There's two things that come out of Warrington, that's really good footballers and beautiful women, which team do you play for?" I got away with it, in fact we thought we were getting on remarkably well with them which boosted our egos, until one of our lads came over with a message from the guy who owned the bar to ask us to see if we could see their 'adams apples?' Yes they were three transvestites.

We were due to play the San Antonio team two days later, with the kick off being arranged for 3 o'clock in the afternoon but on the evening before, two representatives of their club came to our hotel to see us to suggest that we change the kick off time as the weather forecast said it was going to be in the high 90s around that time. They gave us an option of playing at 10.30.a.m. or in the evening, so we chose the earlier kick off time so that it wouldn't interfere with our drinking. By the time their representatives came to see us, many of our lads had already gone out socialising so we told as many as we could that they needed to be in the hotel foyer at 9 in the morning and for them to tell as many of the other players as they could if they saw them in the bars later.

In the morning when we convened, there were about four of our lads, who happened to be the better players, not being there, so myself as manager and the club secretary set about knocking on hotel doors of ladies rooms that we thought our missing players would be in, with the help of the knowledge of who they ended up with the night before from some of the other lads who weren't successful in their plight to end up in an alternative room to which they were booked into, if you get my drift. Eventually, we got together and set off in a supplied coach to the game. Although we had a decent team of players, we got a right tonking 5-0, with the state of some of the players not helping and with the pitch being one of those cinder type that we weren't used to playing on.

I have to say, it was a very enjoyable trip, except I was accused of having my wicked way with one lady by one of the lads which I vehemently denied and by this time, as fun as the trip was, I couldn't wait to get back to my wife. Actually, I was proven not guilty of any such connection with said lady as one of the other players 'pulled' her and acquired a sexually transmitted disease and consequently passed it onto his wife with the relationship with mine blissfully intact.

When we embarked on the plane to come home, the pilot apologised for our delayed take off saying that "He was sorry for the delay, only 'they'd' got held up coming over from France" to which one of the lads responded by shouting "Did they get much?"

Also within our party, was a guy who didn't appear to be connected to anyone , well at least no-one would take responsibility for him. He definitely wasn't one of the players. He was drunk when he got on the plane and was making a right nuisance of himself so much so, that the captain had to come out of his cabin and have a word with him. I remember him saying things like, whilst looking out of the plane window "Look at those people down there, they all look like ants. Oh they are ants we haven't taken off yet." I was also behind him when we left the aircraft when he said to one of the air hostesses "Fucking waste of time that safety demonstration you did wasn't it?" I have to say he was funny.

I got really friendly at The Bull with a fella by the name of Guy, who I am still friendly with to this day, even though I now live in Norfolk and he in Buckhurst Hill on the north-eastern outskirts of London. Guy used to work for Haringey Council and played football for their representative team that played against other London Borough Council teams in a Thursday afternoon league. They were playing Islington Borough Council one afternoon, so I went to the venue in Edmonton to watch the game. I don't think Islington had anybody relatively famous playing for them but Haringey did for them.They had David Gillingwater, the one-time Spurs player who later went to Chelsea who told me once, that he and some Chelsea players went shopping in Oxford Street and he and Terry Venables were pretending that they were holding a sheet of glass both of them with newspapers in their hands to supposedly prevent the pretend glass from cutting them and people were actually walking around them thinking it was all real, this being an idea of Venables's obviously. Haringey also had Jimmy Neighbour in their team, the one-time Spurs Norwich & latterly West Ham player, in fact Jimmy may have still been a West Ham player if a car crash that injured a number of West Ham players who were in the car had occurred a little while earlier. The accident consequently made their squad a bit thin on the ground but alas, Jimmy by then had been released by the club. For all the decent players Haringey had in their team, Islington went into the half-time break leading 2-0.

Roger Morgan, the ex-QPR and Spurs player who couldn't play because of a serious knee injury that finished his career prematurely, was organising the Haringey squad as he worked for the council in a council owned sports hall near the Spurs ground, as did Jimmy Neighbour. Jimmy, whose natural position was as a winger, played the whole of the first half in midfield and as I knew Roger and witnessing that Islington's left back was a real weak link, I suggested to him that Jimmy should come out to the right wing his natural position and' tear their left back to pieces' so that he could get down to the bye-line to cut balls back to the oncoming Haringey players arriving in the penalty box. Roger replied, that all Jimmy wanted to do was 'swan around' in midfield, which made someone present at the game say "It's a shame Jimmy has left West Ham, as he still could have done a decent job for them especially with these injuries that the players had sustained in the car crash" to which Roger responded to by saying, "Yeah, it's alright playing in front of 30 people in a park but it's different to making yourself look a c_ _ _. in front of 30 thousand people in a football stadium," to which this guy Brian said "Well you should know Roger."

Actually, isn't it funny that there seems to be a clone thing going on with the likes of Roger Morgan, Ronnie Wood and Gary Holton, the one-time member of the cast of Auf Wiedersehen Pet and member of the band Heavy Metal Kids who died so tragically early in his life, they all had that drawn scraggy look with black spikey hair in the same way Dennis Law, Rod Stewart, Barry Manilow and Danny Kaye did, high cheek boned with blonde spikey hair, perhaps Danny Kaye not so much.

The Bull pub was a real 'Spurs' pub whereby we organised going to all three of the FA Cup semi-finals that they were in during the 80s in an ex-London Transport double decker bus. We went to Hillsborough for the '81 semi-final v Wolves, where us fans nearly suffered the same fate as the Liverpool fans did in '85. Similar to the Liverpool fans with regards to Forest fans in their game, there were far more Spurs fans than Wolves and we were allocated the Leppings Lane end as were the Liverpool fans. Our coach party entered the Leppings Lane end by the turnstyles to the right of the goal as you look onto the pitch. Although we had terrace tickets to get into the Leppings Lane end behind the goal we couldn't, there just wasn't the room. I and others spent pretty much the whole game being cooped up in a sort of concourse in the corner of the ground not being able to see anything other than when we would run 'up' the wall that was on the end of the long main stand along the side of the pitch where we would hang onto the railings on the top of the wall for a maximum of say five minutes at a time, as you couldn't hang on for any longer.

I have to say in hindsight, I wasn't at all surprised what happped a few years later to the Liverpool fans from what I experienced.

The following 81-2 season , we organised another bus trip from the pub up to Villa Park for the FA Cup Semi-Final versus Leicester City, which we won to help us win the cup again that season. This was to be the Argentinian Ossie Ardiles's last game for Spurs for a couple of seasons, due to the Falklands War before he was shoved over to France to be kept out of the way whilst it went on to play for Paris St. Germain. I made a massive banner which read "Good Luck Ossie, Hurry Up Back" which I unfolded in front of me to drape over the front of the 1st tier of the stand where I was seated in the front row, which the BBC highlighted in their Match Of The Day programme later that evening.

A short while after, my wife and I went over to Marbella to stay with Terry a friend of mine. He was very friendly with Jane Hoad, the daughter of the one-time Australian tennis star Lew Hoad. Jane was married to an Argentinian lad by the name of Alberto, a really sweet and lovely fella. Jane took us to her dad's tennis club that he had up in the hills in Mijas behind Fuengirola to have a game. Unfortunately, we'd only been playing for about half an hour when Lew Hoad himself came down to politely ask us to give up the court as a TV crew had turned up to do an advert. Alberto suggested that my wife and I and Terry should go up to his and Jane's villa further up the hills where he set about to make us a cod cooked in salt lunch. He put the T.V. on and just like a film being shown, was the Falklands War going on. I never could get to grips why we were fighting for this island, what a waste of time and lives and it made it worse by it happening whilst this wonderful man Alberto cooked us lunch. Actually, I felt so humble and guilty whilst he was cooking, I went down to his 'empty' swimming pool to help with scraping off all of the old paint which he had been in the process of doing so that it could be re-painted.

The last FA Cup Semi-Final we went to from The Bull was the 86-7 one against Watford, again at Villa Park, which we won 3-1 to give us the opportunity of taking on Coventry City in the final. All us Spurs fans were behind one of the goals with pretty much Spurs being on the attack for most of the game at the far end to us. Elton John was Chairman of Watford at the time, who by then had let it be well known that he was gay. As said, the ball was consistently at the other end of the pitch but we had a Watford fan that had somehow worked his way into our section of the ground and in his frustration at witnessing Tottenham almost bombarding their goal at the other end shouted "Come on, get it up this end" to which a Spurs fan retorted, "Who said that Elton John."

Around this time my wife and I, moved from Muswell Hill, reluctantly I might add, to Buckhurst Hill on the North East London/Essex border , I say reluctantly, as we loved living at the foot of the 'Ally Pally gates' but the owner of the flat that we were renting wanted to reclaim it back so that his son could move into it after his forthcoming marriage. I was still working for B.T. at the time and on a Saturday if I was working overtime, when finishing I would leave my B.T. van in a depot in Ponders End Enfield and drive home to Buckhurst Hill through the picturesque Epping Forest. The route I would take, would be to drive through the King Edward V reservoirs and then turn left at what was known as the Ching Garage towards Waltham Abbey. About half a mile on the left on the Waltham Abbey road was a pub I used to enjoy drinking in namely The Royal

Oak, owned by Terry Venables but run by his dad Fred who was a lovely old boy but was besotted with everything Terry did. He really thought 'the sun shone out of Terry's proverbial' and why not, he was very proud of what Terry had achieved. It, normally being a Saturday afternoon when I stopped off at the pub, the horseracing was on the telly so that the lads in there could see how their horses fared having had a bet. The pub inside was on a 'split level,' so as to get a decent signal on the old Cathay Ray tube telly as they were then, it was perched on some books that were on a stool which in turn was sat on the top 'split' level of the pub. One afternoon, Fred was out in the kitchen knocking up some cheese and onion rolls for us all to eat. During a break in the horse racing, someone turned the telly channel over which it was on to a channel that was showing a cricket test match between England & Australia. England were doing quite well knocking up a score of around 212 for 2. When Fred came in with a tray of rolls. He looked at the TV and enquired "What's happened to the racing?" With someone in the pub responding by saying "We've just turned it over Fred to see how the cricket was going." Fred then asked "So how are they getting on ?" To which the same guy replied "They're doing OK Fred, they're 212 for 2" Fred straight away responded "Fuck me is Tel batting?" As said it was all about his son Tel. Actually I got on really well with Fred, so much so he asked me if I'd like to go with him out to Barcelona to who Terry was coaching at the time to see Spurs play in a pre-season friendly meeting up afterwards with Terry to go out for dinner. Unfortunately, at the same time the game was on, I, my wife and my friend Guy and his wife were booked to go down to Marbella for a holiday, so I had to unfortunately decline Fred's offer, albeit I did enquire how much it would cost to fly up from Malaga to Barcelona for the game which turned out to be more expensive than it was to fly from London to Malaga, in fact quite considerably so.

A guy named Martin who I got to know when I managed/ran the Arnos football team from The Bull in Edmonton played for 'Old Monovians,' an old boys team made up of ex-pupils of George Monarch School in Walthamstow. As I now lived in Buckhurst Hill, I started to socialise with Martin in their club house on Saturday afternoons which was located in Woodford near Manor Road where Bobby Moore once lived and by Ashton Playing Fields where if you remember from earlier in the book, I played for U.D.T. in the London Banks League when I worked for them. It was also an advantage that Woodford was only a couple of stops on the Central Line to Buckhurst Hill, so it was convenient for me to get home having had a few drinks. Old Monovians had at the time, nine teams with only half of them being at home on any given Saturday, so three would play on the pitches at Woodford with the1st team if they were at home playing on McEntee's schools pitch in Walthamstow because of its tip-top condition in comparison to the Woodford pitches, with any other teams if necessary playing at nearby Wanstead Flats, a sort of miniature Hackney Marshes. At the time I started socialising at the club, anyone who didn't actually attend George Monarchs School wasn't allowed to play for the club albeit this did change gradually, as was the case with many clubs at the time, there were less and less members, which was becoming a problem, most certainly with Monovians and them needing at least 99 players to fill their nine teams.

Eventually I was allowed to play for them, although not before I represented The Gentlemen Of Essex, a team run by the Chairman of Old Monovians Derek Steward, known as Del to one and all. Del had been headmaster at George Monarchs School and was also an after dinner speaker. He was a really funny guy and ran the Gentlemen of Essex as an aside to Old Monovians, as they were a 'Saturday club' with GofE as they were known, playing on Sunday mornings. I was in the clubhouse one

Saturday afternoon after the games had been played when my friend Martin said to me that Del wanted me to play for him the next day. I didn't have a clue who the Gentlemen of Essex were, although I was under the impression that it was a team selected from players all over Essex, in fact all it was was a bunch of eleven blokes that Del knew. Anyway, I felt very privileged to be asked and so I turned out for them. When we got to the game in South London where we were to play the following day, we were getting changed whilst listening to Del's team talk including the line in a very posh voice, "Now lads, don't forget, you're representing the Gentlemen of Essex, so, if you have reason to call the referee a

C _ _ _, don't forget to sound your H's, so don't say 'Ee's a C _ _ _ pronounce the 'H' and say 'He's a C _ _ _." There were another couple of dressing room situations that I was told were attributed to Del although I'm not sure if they were but I'd love to think so, as they were the type of things that he would come out with.

A team that he was in charge of had come off the pitch at half time losing having put in a woeful performance. The players were told to sit down in a circle and he stood in the middle of them pointing to each one in turn in a clockwise direction saying, "You're a C _ _ _, you're a C _ _ _ , you're a C _ _ _ and so on around the team until he came to the fifth player who he pointed at and then left him out but continuing to go round the rest of the team telling them all that they were C _ _ _ s in turn. He then returned to the fella he'd missed out saying "And you, you're a Fucking C _ _ _"

In another situation, he had a go at all the players after they'd lost a game telling them "They were all fucking useless," only for the sub, who was standing by the door and having not been brought on throughout the game to stand there grinning at the abuse his team mates were receiving,

Del looked at him and said "And I don't know what you're fucking laughing at you're not fucking good enough to get into the team." Actually the fact that Del was so well spoken, all the swearing made it sound much funnier.

Having been excepted by the club it wasn't too long before they asked me to run the 'Vets' team. It was great camaraderie in the clubhouse after the games, with the teams that had to play away coming back with some great stories. In fact this for me was where all the fun really started. Some of the stories were just hilarious. There was a game, where one of the teams were playing away and the home team didn't have a ref, so the opposition sent one of their representatives over to a pub opposite their ground to see if they had a whistle or something that the stand-in referee could use to attract the players attention with when making a decision. He returned with a metal tray and a wooden spoon which somehow did the trick. There was another occasion when one of our teams played over at Wanstead Flats. One of our players was late getting to the game, arriving about five minutes before the game kicked off. As he ran into the dressing room, he met the ref coming out with a white mac on and his ref's tunic underneath it. He said to the ref "Is it off?" To which the ref replied "No, go and get changed I'll be back shortly." Sure enough the ref came back about ten minutes later, put his mac in the dressing room and started the game. There were some quite rumbustious tackles going in right from the start not being met with any bookings or anything. All of a sudden a number of yobs appeared on the horizon making their way down to where the game was being played. They were on the touchline giving the ref some abuse when a foul was committed nowhere near as bad as ones that had gone on previously. The ref called over the offending player and said something in his ear at the same time brandishing a red card. The player left the field of play as quick as he could, with the remaining ten players of his team getting around the ref saying "Why did you send him off for that, there's been far worse tackles being committed before and you didn't do anything about them." To which the ref replied "Just leave it and get on with the game." With that, about five minutes or so later, the place was swarming with police cars. What happened was, when he left the dressing room just before the kick off, he'd answered a call and went to a block of flats nearby where there had been a disturbance There were other officers that answered the call as well so he left them to it and returned to ref the game but the louts that had been causing the disturbance recognised him as they made their way across the football pitches, so on his perception that things could turn nasty he sent the lad off telling him to go to a phone box to call 999 and tell them what was happening, Clever eh?

One lad I remember, played for Old Monovians on a Saturday afternoon went into the bar afterwards and stayed the evening, got too drunk to go home to his wife and crashed out in a friends flat. The next morning, he didn't go home either, he went and played for his Sunday League team but during the game his wife came onto the pitch with his Sunday roast dinner and threw it at him.

On another occasion, one of Monovians teams were playing a team by the name of Foresters Old Boys. Their ground was adjacent to the Central Underground Line somewhere between Theydon Bois and Epping, a part of the 'line' that was overground not underground. They had quite a few pitches and the game was to take place on one of the furthest pitches from the dressing rooms, which took about 10 minutes to walk to. It was a real murky February Saturday afternoon with a two o'clock kick off, with the lights on the houses up on the hills already on and flickering in the grey of the afternoon. The referee called the captains together for the toss and then said "Fuck it," to which one of the captains said "What's up ref?" The referee replied that he'd left his watch in his trousers back in the locker, one of which he and all the players were allocated in the dressing room. He said that he'd have to go to get it, to which the home side's captain said "You can't do that ref, it'll take you 10 minutes to go back there, 5 minutes to get into your locker and rummage through your trousers and then 10 minutes to get back here, that's almost half n' hour,' it'll be nearly 4.30 when we finish the game, it'll be dark by then" With that a voice 'piped up' "Ref, I think I can help you." The ref replied "Oh yeah and how do you think you can help me, have you got a watch?" The fella replied "No but I work for London Transport and I know that those Central Line trains, (pointing to the rail tracks by the side of the pitches), run every 15 minutes, so if we kick off when the next one comes along, in three trains time it'll be half time 45 minutes, then we can turn straight round and play another three trains worth of 45 minutes" which the referee agreed to and was grateful of.

There were other funny stories e.g. the referee who sat in his car all the game because it was pouring down with rain and blew his horn when he wanted to give a foul and switched his indicator on to indicate to which team he'd given the decision to but the funniest story though involved the captain of Monovians 9th team. He came back to the clubhouse from a game having taken place on Wanstead Flats. Someone asked him how they'd got on, to which he replied "It was a fucking disaster." "Why, what happened?" someone drinking his beer at the bar asked .

The captain replied "About 11 o'clock this morning, the appointed referee rang up to tell me he couldn't make it. So I got to the ground about one o'clock with about three of our of lads turning up just shortly after." He explained to them what the problem was so between them, they came up with the idea that the last player to turn up would have to referee, with perhaps one of the other players injured or otherwise taking over from him for the second half, either way, they were only going to play with 10 men as substitutes weren't allowed in their league at the time. The opposition had arrived, so 'our' captain went to their captain to explain the situation and to ask them did they still want to play, to which their captain replied in the affirmative saying that they'd travelled over two hours to get there from Croydon South

West London. The last Monovian player to arrive was a school teacher, who was told of the circumstances and how they came to the decision as to who should referee. He wasn't best pleased but agreed to do it albeit saying "I haven't a whistle though. "The Monovians captain took him to the opposition's dressing room to introduce him to them at the same time telling them he didn't have a whistle, which none of the opposition did either. Their captain asked how then would he alert the players that he wanted to give a decision, to which he replied "I'll shout stop!" To which their captain enquired "Yes but what if the player in possession of the ball is say running down the line on the far side of the pitch and the ball goes out of play and he makes out he can't hear you?" To which the volunteering referee replied: "I'll shout stop C _ _ _ !"

I wrote in to Danny Kelly and John Inverdale when they were doing the Radio 5 'Drive In' programme many years ago, as they loved anecdotal stories being sent into them, requesting that if they were to tell it over the air they should do so at 5 o'clock on a Friday afternoon, as I knew I would be home by then. It was only a week later when I got home from work to the Pink Cottage in which my wife, daughter and I lived that I turned the radio on in the event they told the story, not believing that they would, what with the 'blue' language in it. The 5 o'clock news was read and then Danny Kelly said "Right, we have a story from a John in Norfolk and it says a lot for John in as much as he lives in a Pink' cottage." He then went onto relay the story with me saying to my wife "He can't read this out" as it was written with the 'C' word in it. As it went on, when Danny Kelly got to the point where it said "And what will you do if the fella who's in possession of the ball is running down the line on the far side of the pitch and it goes out of play and he makes out he can't hear you and carries on running?" Danny changed it and said, "I'll shout stop you bastard" which actually sounded funnier. The story must have been entertaining, as it made the following Saturday's Telegraph in one of the sports journalist's column.

Some of the Old Monovians lads actually taught at the McEntee School in Walthamstow where the 1st team played their home games which was I guess how they were allowed to play there. A couple of the lads I got friendly with, namely Mick and a chap who had the nickname Poundsy, asked me if I'd referee a game between the teachers at their McEntee School and teachers from another local school which I took time off work early in agreement to do. I was told before the game, there was likely to be at the least animosity between the two sets of players but what ensued was incredible, they were kicking the shit out of each other. In one incident about an hour into the game Poundsy, who was folically challenged himself, got into a fracas with one of the oppositions players and called him a C_ _ _ ! leaning over him whilst he was on the ground. I said to all the players by then "look, I've taken time off work to ref this game so if you're going to carry on like this I'm off to the Crooked Billett pub over the road and you can sort this out yourselves." They all agreed that things would cool down, so I told Poundsy to go over and apologise to the recipient of him calling him what he did. So Poundsy went over and said to the lad, who was also folically challenged, "I'm sorry, I didn't mean to call you a C_ _ _ I meant to call you a Bald C_ _ _ ! That was it, off I went to the pub and let them get on with it.

What with me living in Buckhurst Hill and the two aforementioned guys Mick and Poundsy and others living in Loughton, we used to drink in The Carpenters Arms in Smarts Lane in which the Loughton Police Station was situated. After a while, a few of us got together in the pub and formed a Sunday morning team, which again I was asked to run/manage. I have to say, it was a very well run club which we named The Carpenters Arms with around 60% of the playing personnel being either from the Metropolitan Police and Essex Constabulary, as many of the old bill out of Loughton Police Station drank in there, which helped us get our home pitch on The Police Sports Ground in Chigwell, right opposite where Alan Sugar lived.

We had some real characters playing for us, not least our left back Johnny Glasscock, not a great footballer by his own admission but a 100% committed one, who endearingly acquired the nickname of 'peanut' as he was always getting roasted. I remember him saying in a game once when things weren't going too well, "Lads, JR (that's me) said that the game should be simple not the players." When we were set up and ready to go, we went up to Scarborough for a pre-season bonding weekend. One of the lads who was in the police force, had connections with the police up in Yorkshire and arranged for us to play a couple of games against them, one being at the McCain Oven Chips Sports Ground, I can't remember where the other one was. We had a committee meeting to organise the arrangements, the first thing being on the agenda was how we got up there. I decided that we needed to all go together not in separate cars, as all being together was part of the bonding process. We enquired as to the cost of a small coach, say 18-22 seater with a driver but 'they' wanted somewhere in the region of £750. which was a little out of our budget, so I then I asked if anyone in our party had a PSV license to drive the coach which would get the cost down but no-one did. I then suggested again, so that we all travelled together, we go by train, which made some joker perk up with "Don't be a c _ _ _ John, we can't get anyone to drive the coach how are we gonna get anyone to drive the fucking train?" True.

So, we set off for the weekend in a mini-bus that we hired, with a few of us taking it in turn to drive. We arrived on a Friday evening and stayed in a hotel that backed onto Scarborough's cricket ground. The next day, when we were due to play our first game against the Yorkshire police, all police leave was called off so was consequently our game as Scarborough were playing their first home game of the season against Wolves having been promoted from The Conference League. Consequently we were all at a loose end during the Saturday, the only saving grace being that a Michael Parkinson's eleven were playing a Viv Richards World eleven on the cricket ground behind the hotel that we were staying in that started at 10.30 in the morning that we could all sit on our veranda and watch. The lads decided as it was a nice day, later they'd all go down to the beach in the afternoon and have a game of football. Although I was 'manager,' I was still able to play but I was just getting over a ligament injury in my ankle as was my friend of Guy who, as I said I'd got very friendly with in The Bull pub many years ago, who I was sharing a room with who, incidentally, was a dead ringer for the Newcastle born Sting. He and I decided that we didn't want to hang around all day not being able to partake in the beach football, so it being the opening day of the league's season and being massive Spurs fans, we decided we'd go to see them play their opening game up at Newcastle, which wasn't that far away from Scarborough. We got a train to York and then the main line express up to Newcastle. When we arrived at the station, we asked a copper where their ground St. James's Park was but he said "Are you with the Spurs Supporters Club or on your own?" To which we replied "On our own." So he said to us that the ground wasn't that far from the station if you walked through the city centre but he then went on to say that he wouldn't do that if he were us with Guy looking so much like Sting, as we'd go past the pubs and the Newcastle fans would all want to talk to him and if we opened our cockney mouths and they then realise it wasn't him anything could happen. So he suggested we should wait for the supporters trains to arrive in about half n' hour and then be escorted up with them. So, we were standing there when all the Spurs fans alighted from the train. Now, do you remember earlier in the book when I said I sat next to a guy on the plane on the way back from seeing Spurs play Real Madrid in Spain? Well he was amongst them and came up to me and said "Wotcha, how you doing?

You come up on the supporters club train?" To which I replied "Nah, our Sunday league team has got a game in Scarborough tomorrow morning so we've taken the opportunity of coming here via York this afternoon." To which he replied, "Your Sunday morning team? That's some sort of fucking Sunday league you're in innit playing away in Scarborough?" So off we all set off for the ground, me and my friend Guy mingling in the middle of them so that no-one would recognise him. It was a great experience. it was Gazza'a debut for Tottenham and he got pelted with Mars Bars referring to his weight. It was all done in good humour, a 2-2 draw if I remember was the result and then we returned to Scarborough in time to meet up with the lads and go out on the lash with them in the evening.

The next day, we played the second organised game which was still on as said at McCains Sports Ground. It really was something else, in fact many professional teams that would have to travel up to the North East would use the facilities to train there before a game. I was standing on the touchline during the game next to our club chairman, when our team got a throw in. One of our players Del took the throw yelling at the same time "Colin!" with the ball going straight to one of the opposition which made our Chairman say "That's clever Del how did you know his name?"

Back in Loughton, we did ok in our 1st season in our local Sunday league, better than we thought we would, as the club was only set up as a social thing because of us all drinking in the pub together. As said previously, because of the number of police personnel in the team we were able to play our home games at the local Chigwell Police Sports Ground all except on one occasion, when we had to transfer a home game to the council owned Avondale Recreation Ground as there was a police dog show at the police sports ground. At the police sports ground, I suppose by definition, there was never any problems with the players personal belongings being stolen, in fact I don't remember the dressing rooms being locked whilst we were playing but at Avondale, the dressing rooms were never locked so we had to take the players personal belongings out onto the pitch with us which we did in a sock which our keeper put in the net of his goal for safekeeping. Unfortunately, the sock was stolen whilst the game was in progress with bundles of money and expensive watches in it. The funny thing was though in the pub afterwards, the talk wasn't about the sock and its contents it was the fact that one of the players only had one sock on.

Loughton in the 80s when the club was formed, was quite an exciting place to live. We had some great pubs that we used to frequent amongst others in the town, The Carpenters Arms that the football club was formed in, The Gardeners that was high up at the top of York Hill where you could get a great view of the City of London and Canary Wharf from, The Foresters that overlooked Epping Forest and Bensons Winebar that all the 'trendies' went to including myself and my wife which was just along the way from our boutique Sloppy Joe's in Loughton High Road

Not too long after, our daughter Charley came along and my wife and I and two other couples and their newly born daughters, three mums, twelve of us in total hired out a thatched roof cottage in Norfolk for ten days over Christmas in 1990. Incidentally, if you remember, Andy Warhol once said "Everyone's going to have 15mins of fame," well our daughter's was being born in the same hospital as David Beckham, Whipps Cross in Wanstead. We had a great time in Norfolk and my wife Steph and I felt so comfortable there that we decided when we got back to London to sell up and move there, contrary to what Dr Johnson said "If you're fed up with London you're fed up with life" so I guess we must have been. I always wanted to live in Spain but my wife wasn't so keen but I think she did want to fulfil the spirit of her dad who, having travelled all around the world as a Royal Navy and merchant seaman always wanted to end his days in Norfolk albeit unfortunately, not doing so before he passed away. So I suppose it was a compromise for me and a decision that we made to move our daughter out of London before she grew up to realise what we had done to her, but her now saying that although she was born Essex/London, she has always considered herself a Norfolk girl.

For my part, I think many people thought I was going on the run or something, as everybody was thinking of me in the old adage of 'You can take the boy out of the city but you can't take the city out of the boy,' which I must still admit is true with me.

I remember the day we moved, it was a Monday 8th April 1991. I remember it clearly, as on the following Wednesday the 10th Spurs were playing Norwich at Carrow Road with Paul Gascoigne making a comeback having been out injured for a while to prove his fitness, so as to play in the upcoming F.A.Cup Semi-Final on the following Sunday. We lost the Norwich game 2-1, Ian Crook scoring the winner for Norwich to get his own back for Tottenham letting him go. Actually, Ian Crook was a very underrated player, he was so unlucky to have such good players in the Spurs squad similar to him such as Hoddle, Ardiles and Hazard. I went to the game on my own thinking I could get a ticket quite easily but I couldn't get into the area where the Spurs fans were because Norwich wouldn't sell tickets for the Spurs 'away' end and I couldn't buy a ticket in the home end as I didn't have proof of a home address in Norfolk, so I went round to the main entrance to see if there were any touts that I could get one from. As I walked up to it, I saw some lads outside who I knew from my drinking days in the British Queen in Tottenham, a couple of them being fellow telephone engineers when I was one. They asked me if I had a ticket, saying they had a spare, as one of them was Mandy Smith's uncle, she being the one-time wife of The Rolling

Stone's Bill Wyman but was now going out with Pat Van Den Hauwe the Spurs full back who was playing on the night who had given them the tickets. They said the only condition was, was that I had to go into the players lounge with them after the game, so a double result then. They then went onto ask me if I'd driven to the game on my own to which I replied "Yeah, it only took me 20mins." One of them replied "Only 20 minutes from Tottenham, what sort of fucking car are you driving?" I then had to explain that I'd moved to live in Norfolk but they couldn't believe it, as I said a few paragraphs ago, they were of the impression that I was of the adage 'You can take the boy out of the city but not the city out of the boy,' they were flabbergasted that I of all people had moved up to Norfolk.

No sooner did I move to Norfolk, than I was back down in London within a week to witness Gascoigne score that wondrous free kick against The Arsenal that won us the aforementioned F.A. Cup semi-final.

When I moved to Norfolk I got a job working for The Sun Life Of Canada, selling life insurance and pensions and although I was quite good at working with figures, it was something I had no previous knowledge or experience in. Myself and the younger lads in the office in Norwich, talked about football at every opportunity which annoyed one of the senior older men Vic, who had no interest in football whatsoever. One day he said to me, "John, if you knew as much about this business as you do about football you'd be the top salesman earning a lot of money." A little while after I had to do a presentation of some aspect in terms of what the company were able to offer in the field of finance and I thought perhaps there was something in what old Vic had said, football not being that far detached from selling financial services. So on the day of the presentation I got a flip chart and on it I put photos of the Leeds United players of the 60s/70s that included the likes of Alan Clarke, Peter Lorimer,

Norman Hunter Johnny Giles & Billy Bremner, albeit above them I wrote LEADS UNITED as I went on to explain, that salesmen were dependent on 'leads' in getting in touch with people to sell them a product. I explained that as in football "You have good leads and bad leads" drawing a ring around Giles, Hunter & Bremner saying that they were 'bad LEEDS.' I went onto explain that again as in football, you need a strategy as to how you play and as to how you deal with a client e.g. you need to attack when necessary but also you need to be defensive and listen to the client when necessary and being lethal with your finishing in terms of the end of a move in football or closing a sale with regards to selling the client a product. I even went onto say that in football, you have a referee as you do in Financial Services which at the time was the FSA (Financial Services Authority), which was there to see fair play between the client and the company selling a product.

Actually it went down really well, with my manager, who was by coincidence a Leeds fan taking it to our area manager to show him who in turn, asked me if they could use it nationwide which they did.

As much as I enjoyed working for Sun Life of Canada, I left within six months, as the company policy was if you stayed with the company for longer than that you could have any commissions rescinded if a client reneged on a product that you sold them and they didn't keep up their payments. I decided to resign mainly because I was out most evenings seeing prospective clients and I was missing my young daughter growing up, notwithstanding that up here in North Norfolk where I was working it was difficult to find the addresses of houses up country lanes that you had to go to in the dark, no Twat Navs in those days.

One of my clients was the wife of a very successful building company owner and I remember going round to their house one Tuesday evening. After giving the wife the lowdown as to how her pension was performing, their two sons, who were only about eight years old at the time, were watching Hibs playing Celtic on SKY and on asking me if I liked football they invited me to sit and watch it with them. I'd not been long appointed the Youth Academy Scout for East Anglia for Tottenham, the appointment of which is explained later in the book. This really grabbed the attention of the two boys and the dad Dick Cooper, a really lovely guy and we spoke for ages watching the game and talking football generally. It turned out that Dick was Chairman of Overstrand Football Club up on the coast next to Cromer and he invited me along to see them play. Their ground was really quaint, them sharing it with the relatively successful cricket club which included a wonderful old club house with a thatched roof. Overstrand were a good football team for the level that they were playing at and about the time got drawn away in the semi-final of the Norfolk Senior Cup to Diss Town, a good side themselves having won the F.A. Vase around the time. Dick asked me if I wanted to go to the game, saying that the team coach would pick me up at the top of my road at the junction of the A140, which is the main road from Cromer to Norwich which we had to travel along to get to Diss which was on the southern side of the city. Unfortunately, Diss were too good for Overstrand being a level or so above them, in fact if I remember, Diss went onto winning the trophy beating Wroxham in the final. The other unfortunate thing for Overstrand, was that shortly after, they had to give up their shared partnership of the ground on which they played as I believe the cricketing half of it didn't want them there anymore, so they had to 'jump in bed' with Mundesley, another adjacent village team to form MADRA (Mundesley & District Recreation Association) which was never the same.

The good thing is though, that I still see one of the brothers Jed, even though he's now in his 30s now. In fact I've met up with him in Fuengirola in Spain on a couple of occasions, as he's organised golfing trips out there with another ten or so lads from our local Aylsham market town whilst I was out there visiting my friend who lives there.

Now here's a funny anecdote about Diss Town Football Club, well at least I think it is so there.

It involved the nuclear power station that is Sizewell B in Suffolk. They wanted to form a football team and in doing so they tried to arrange some pre-season friendlies for the newly formed team to play in. Their secretary got in touch with the secretary of Diss Town F.C. situated in Norfolk, who at the time weren't a bad side, in fact the season previously '93-4, they had won the FA Vase at Wembley as previously said. The Sizewell B secretary explained to the Diss Town secretary why he was calling, to ask if they could play them in a pre-season friendly, which the Diss Town secretary agreed to do, albeit saying to the Sizewell B secretary "Sorry, who are you again?" To which he replied "Sizewell B ." To which the Diss Town secretary said "Well I think you'd better send your 'A' team as we're quite a good side you know." He obviously didn't know what Sizewell 'B' was.

Football wise having moved up to Norfolk, I was 'like a fish out of water.' Having played all my life, I didn't know anyone at the time to get a game with, so I decided I'd take a referee's course at the University of East Anglia. One evening, we were in the classroom when the subject was about getting players back 10 yards from a free-kick. We had two instructors and they were trying to put over the deception of how far 10 yards was from where a kick was taken. They were at one end of the classroom and they were asking us how long along the central aisle in the classroom 10 yards was, with trainees pointing to the floor saying where they thought it would be. To prove the deception, one of the instructors stood at the front of the classroom holding one end of an orange nylon rope, whilst the other proceeded to take the rope along the aisle to the 'breeze-blocked' wall at the far end of the room. I have to say, they did prove a point as the instructor holding the end of the rope, put it up against the wall with a metre or so of it still hanging down to the floor and so I said as you would, "Well move the wall back then," God, you could have heard a pin drop with regards to the two instructors, the rest of the class were laughing their heads off. It was one of those things that if the instructors didn't crack the jokes they weren't funny, pretty much like the instructors at a speeding awareness course if you've attended one. No? You were lucky then I thought everybody had.

I started to referee in the North Norfolk League in the October of the next season having got through the examination. I quite enjoyed it, the only aspects of it that I didn't enjoy was that if you upset one of the teams they wouldn't speak to you in the bar afterwards nor would the other team because they didn't want to upset their opponents, so in effect, you were ostracised and left on your own or, as what happened to me was, one of the home team said to me "Ref, do you want a drink?" To which I replied "Actually it's John, my name's John" to which he replied "OK ref what do you want to drink?" That was the problem you completely lost your self identity as a ref.

I only booked one lad from October through to March and that was because he called me a C - – -. I suppose I really should have sent him off but I was a trappy sod when it came to referees when I played, so I was a bit lenient with him. I told him that I was refereeing because I was too old to play and so I took up refereeing so as to put something back into the game in return for the pleasure it had given me over the years but I drew the line at giving up my Saturday afternoon so that I could be verbally abused by a little runt like him. Actually, he was quite impressed with what I said and apologised profusely.

The only thing was, the Referees Secretary pulled me to one side when we had the referees assessment meeting at the end of the season to ask me why I only booked one player all season, to which I replied, "I didn't find it necessary to give out anymore bookings but if there was a minimum requirement per season you should have told me." He replied by saying, "No, don't get me wrong John I was just curious." I don't think that was really the case as I later was told that the North Norfolk League came under the jurisdiction of the Norfolk F.A. which was a Plc and autonomous from funding from the Football Association, so they were 'allegedly' dependent on fines applied to bookings and sendings off to run themselves.

The other thing that happened during my relatively short tenure as a referee, was when I refereed a match in a Norfolk village called Trunch which looks as it sounds.

The F.A. had just brought in the rule of the 'professional foul,' whereby a 'last' defender that commits a foul against an attacking player of the opposition should be sent off that was already in place in the professional game would also be brought into 'junior' lower league football. I was dreading having to carry out the law, so before the game I went into both teams dressing rooms in order to make them aware of the rule and to prevent me from being embarrassed if I did have to send someone off. As I walked into the home team dressing room, I was welcomed with a shout of "Johnny Ray" from one of the players. As I looked round to the area from which it had come, there was only a guy by the name of Dave Speck who I'd played with all those 25 years ago when I played with him for the All Saints Teachers Training College in Tottenham where he had done his teachers training. I must admit, we had a bit of a hug but not insight of the away team. Shortly into the game, Dave scored a perfectly good goal and went running back to the centre circle celebrating but as he did so, I blew my whistle awarding a free kick against him for offside. Well, the verbal abuse I received from him was dreadful but I let him carry on until I was ready to tell him that I was only joking and retracted my decision, to which he replied "You bastard Johnny Ray" for which I sent him off, no not really. We had a good laugh about it as did all the other players on the pitch especially the away team, who had no idea what was going on. Incidentally, it was lucky the Referee's Secretary didn't get wind of it as I would have been in deep pooh pooh.

I didn't have to continue my involvement in refereeing into the next season, as I was asked by the football team in my adjoining village Felmingham to play for them. I was about 50 at the time but I was just pleased that I could still play to some degree. The thing that impressed me, was that in lower league football in London, unless you played in an 'Old Boys' or 'Banks' league whereby every club had their own ground, very often you would play on pitch No. 4 at home on say a place like Hackney Marshes one week and on pitch 104 as an away fixture the next. In the North Norfolk league in which Felmingham played, it was pretty much made up of village teams, that all had their own pitches and bar. I remember we were in the bar after a home game when our centre half Kevin, who like me moved up from London albeit many years before, asked our manager who we'd got the next week, with the reply being East Ruston. Kevin replied "Oh no we haven't have we?" I said to Kev "Why, what's wrong with playing there Kev?" To which he replied "12 years I've played in this league and I've never won there." It was equivalent to Spurs not having won at Anfield from 1912, the year the Titanic sank, to when 72 years later, Garth Crook scored a winner in a

1-0 victory, as I explained earlier in the book when I met Spurs centre-forward Bobby Smith.

After a game in the bar, I once brought up the subject of, having been there and done it myself, players being ungrateful as to the thousands of people who give up their time to run junior league football teams, saying that the players just turn up on a match day and expect everything to be in place so that they can play, some even wanting their boots laced by the manager. The guy who was our manager and the overall organiser of our club, was a wonderful Scottish bloke by the name of Billy, who was quintessential in the type of person I was trying to describe. Someone then likened Billy to a guy who ran another village side close by to us by the name of Erpingham, which was run by for many years by a guy by the name of Stuart, saying he used to pick the team and ring the players to let them know they were playing, cut the grass and mark it out on a Friday before a home game, sometimes playing himself if they were short and on occasions, even referee a game whilst he was playing if the ref didn't turn up, to which someone added in the bar "Yeah and he gave himself offside once."

A funny story about the East Ruston football club, involved a neighbour of mine David who is around the same age as me. He once told me, that when he played for the club some 50 years ago, they got through to the quarter-finals of a national cup competition and that they were drawn away to a team in Sussex, which was obviously many miles from Norfolk with the networking of major roads not being as accessible as they are now. They went down in a 60 seater coach with some of the fans who went with them sitting on beer crates along the aisle of the coach. He said it took them ages, with one of the guys who was sitting uncomfortably on a crate throughout the journey saying "I didn't know you could go this far." Typical Norfolk humour.

Just after I joined the Felmingham football team, a guy who was running the village's U-13 team asked me if I'd help coach them on the basis that he'd heard I'd played at a decent level with Barnet and Leyton. We had a kiddie by the name of Danny Tindall, he was some player for his age. We weren't a particularly good team, there just wasn't the talent in the village and surrounding ones, what really good lads there were went off to play for nearby market towns like North Walsham & Aylsham if that is, they weren't good enough for Norwich City's academy. How Danny remained with us I don't know. He was a striker and he would score a hat-trick almost every game, so we left him up front to do his stuff and build the team defensively in numbers around him. Because of Danny's ability to score goals, any team that we played had to score three to get a draw, which many did and more unfortunately. I felt so strongly that Danny had a special talent I wrote to Tottenham Hotspur F.C. to ask them what they did with regards to recommendations up in Norfolk and to my surprise and astonishment, I received a letter back signed by the one and only Ossie Ardiles, who was the manager at the time, inviting me down to their training ground to see how they operated and to have a chat.

So a couple of weeks later, off I went with Nicky, the son of Billy who ran the Felmingham mens team. Nicky, who was only 14 himself, had never been outside Norfolk let alone gone to London. As we got nearer to London around the M25 to Mill Hill where the training ground was at the time, whilst Chigwell was being built having been evicted from their previous training ground in Cheshunt which had been sold for housing, the weather was getting worse and worse, getting to 'monsoon' status by the time we arrived. Getting into the training ground was like trying to get into Fort Knox. The 'jobsworth' on the gate was most awkward in letting us in until I produced my letter of invitation from Ossie, in fact, when he saw it he couldn't open the gates quick enough, almost 'tugging his furlock' as he did . Luckily, I had a large umbrella with us, so we got out of the car and walked over to the side of the pitch to watch the first team training. Ossie was in the middle of the pitch talking to the players who weren't best happy being out there with the weather as it was. Soon, Stevie Perryman, who was Ossie Ardiles's assistant was putting out some cones, came over and asked us what we were doing there. Again I presented him with Ossie's letter, so Stevie said

"As you can see, it's not a good day, what I suggest you do is when you get back to Norfolk, phone the club and ask to speak to John Moncur who was head of the Academy, as I understand we're looking for a scout in East Anglia."

I couldn't wait to get back home to make the call but Nicky was looking forward to going to White Hart Lane to take some photos with his camera, so we called in there on the way home. On arrival, the guy on the gate, similar to the one at Mill Hill wouldn't allow us in but luckily, I knew a guy named Jimmy who was head of stadium security when I was living in Tottenham before I moved up to Norfolk and convinced the gate guy to get hold of him for me having found out that he was still at the club. Whilst we were standing there waiting, Stevie Perryman turned up in his BMW as training I assume had, been cancelled due to the weather. When he recognised us he said, "That was quick, have you phoned the club already?" I told him no and that I was waiting for Jimmy to let us into the ground so Stevie said "Oh come on then" and took us into the ground and onto the pitch so that Nicky could take his photos. As we left to go to the car, we passed the first team dressing room where I noticed Stevie sitting on the treatment bed talking to someone, so I put my head round the door and thanked him to which he responded "No problem John and don't forget to make that call."

As everybody knows, Stevie Perryman was a great devotee to Tottenham and a great player. I met a girl in 1970 in Campastilla, a seaside resort in Majorca, Babs I think her name was. When we got back to England, she invited me up to Pudsey in Yorkshire where she lived, the town that the bear in the BBC's Children In need programme is named after. I took up her invitation but I coincided it with Spurs playing nearby Leeds United. Leeds were to say the least, a very physical side at the time not least being urged on by their baying fans to 'Get some blood on yer boots.'

Stevie was only young at the time and played in it almost spending the whole game marking Johnny Giles out of the game. Spurs won 2-1 and I remember at the end of the game, Johnny

Giles in his frustration, aimed a few choice words at Stevie with Stevie replying with the old 'Nescafe Hand Shuffle.' When I got on the train at Kings Cross to go up there, I noticed the TV presenter Cliff Michelmore with a TV crew. I realised a couple of months later that they too were going up to Leeds on the train to shoot some footage that they intended to use on a programme at the time called 'So You Think You Can Believe Your Eyes.' It was a programme whereby they showed you something on the screen and then asked you a question about it, in this case it was whether Spurs Martin Chivers was in the penalty area or outside it when he scored the winning goal.

Actually, I didn't exactly use girls that lived some distance from me on purpose but for some reason, most of them I went to visit by coincidence revolved around football. I went out with a girl from Brentford and when I went over to her house, which backed onto Brentford's Griffin Park, she took me out into the back garden where she showed me about half a dozen footballs that had been kicked over the advertising KLM Airways roofed stands. I remember another girl Lyn who my friends and I, whilst returning back to Tottenham from Clacton-on-Sea, gave a lift to along with her friend who we saw 'thumbing it' on the side of the road for a lift back to a place called Tiptree where the famous jam is made where they lived. I got her phone number and started up a bit of a relationship with her, with her coming down to Tottenham and me going up to hers at weekends

One weekend I went to visit her arriving on the Friday evening. The next day the Saturday, Colchester United were playing Plymouth Argyle, the club I had a lot of affiliation for because of my dad's brother living down there in Devon, so I thought I'd take the opportunity of going along to Layer Road Colchester's old ground and watch it returning to Lyn's house afterwards to go out in the evening. It was a freezing cold afternoon with the pitch so frozen I was surprised that the game went ahead. Anyway it did and during the game, a young Colchester full back ventured on an overlap near to where I was standing and found himself chasing a hopeless ball down towards the oppositions corner flag. The opposing Plymouth full back had reached the ball before the young Colchester full back but found himself penned in by the corner flag by the now flagging Colchester full back with the ball stopping so as not to go out of play. The Plymouth full back must have thought, the only way to get out of this was to 'hoof' the ball right at the nuts of his opponent which he did. Now anyone who's been on the receiving end of something like that knows full well that it's painful at the best of times but when it's freezing cold even moreso. I was standing next to some fellas who I'd got chatting to and one of them said, "That'll put paid to his 'fun' tonight," referring to the young Colchester player who was the recipient of the kicked ball, to which another guy who was standing within earshot of it butting in to say "I hope so, he's seeing my daughter tonight and that'll put paid to any intentions he may have."

The next day I had Sunday lunch with Lyn and her family and fell asleep afterwards on a settee. Unknowingly, she tied the shoelaces of both my shoes together and when I woke up and went to go to the loo I fell arse over tit and smashed the glass coffee table. Oh well, the relationship was good while it lasted.

As soon as I got home from my trip down to the Mill Hill training ground, as said, I couldn't wait to make the call to John Moncur the Head of Spurs Academy albeit unfortunately, I'd found out that Danny Tindall, who was the catalyst for me to write to Tottenham, had moved to Nottingham, as his mum and dad had split up and he went with his dad back to from where he came. I later found out that Danny had had trials with Forest and Lincoln City and I was told later that he'd signed for Ajax in Holland. I don't know if that was true though, I hope it was.

I went back down to Tottenham to have two interviews with John Moncur, a really great fella who was, as you could describe in those days, as being 'black & white' with what you saw you got. He was also the father of John Moncur the one-time Spurs, Swindon & West Mam player. At my second interview, John appointed me as the East Anglia Academy Scout. I felt so privileged and proud having supported the club for around 40 plus years, the trouble was, I had to move to Norfolk to do it ironically.

A few weeks later, I returned to London to attend my first scouts meeting at the new training ground now in Chigwell to be introduced to my fellow scouts, one of them being to my astonishment Dickie Moss, the one-time headmaster of Rowland Hill School who I mentioned right at the beginning in the book, who gave me my very first game for Tottenham Boys all those years ago. Dickie was as surprised as I was when he greeted me, giving me a big hug on seeing me. John Moncur asked me how I knew Dickie and then proceeded in telling me an anecdote, one that I relayed onto Norfolk lads who played for Norfolk County Schools who I coached for some years to instil into them, that wanting to be a professional footballer was not just about ability but just as importantly if not moreso, 'Desire.'

John said that Dickie came into his office one Thursday and said to him, that he had seen this 12 year old kiddie play and that they should both go and watch him. John said to Dickie that he was rather busy at the time but Dickie insisted, saying that "We ought to go sooner rather than later as the lad was in great demand and they might lose out on him." John then relented and asked Dickie when he intended to go and have another look to which Dickie replied "At his next school's game in Chingford the following Saturday morning." So, off they both went and when they got there John asked Dickie who was the kiddie they were to look at. Dickie replied "This blonde lad coming over to take the corner kick" where they were both standing. John said, looking at the lads skinny legs "He won't be able to reach this side of the penalty area with those legs let alone the far side" even though it was only a junior sized pitch not a full size one. Dickie replied "Oh yeah? Just you wait and see" and with that without hardly any backlift, the lad hit the ball to the far side of the penalty area. They left the game with John admitting that they would "have to keep tabs on him." A few weeks later, the lad's school went over to Barcelona on a trip around the Nou Camp with him in their party. Whilst they were there, the lads from the school were invited to partake in a 'keepy-uppey' competition along with lads from Barcelona schools and a school from Portugal, with the lad that Dickie had found winning it. Terry Venables was coach at Barca at the time, being in attendance at the competition, however he was soon dismissed by the club and returned to England to manage Spurs not long after. Directly he arrived at White Hart Lane, he called John Moncur out, asking if the lad who won the competition that he witnessed was with any professional club and if not, with Chingford being relatively local to Tottenham why not Tottenham. John called Dickie straight away telling him that TV as Terry Venables, was known, wanted the lad at the club and that as Dickie knew the family he should go round there and convince him to come to Tottenham. By this time, although the lad couldn't sign for anyone until he was 14 years of age, as was the ruling at the time, Dickie had been told that the lad had his heart on signing for Manchester United to which John replied "Well has he signed for them?" To which Dickie responded in the negative for John to say "Well then get him to come here." So off Dickie went to the family's house thinking he had a good chance of coaxing the lad to Tottenham as the lad's grandfather was a season ticket holder at Spurs and a devoted fan. The mum and dad just repeated what Dickie already knew, that their son had his heart set on signing for United but as the lad was only 12 and a half years of age at the time and not being able to sign even if he was good enough, Dickie suggested that a compromise should be reached so that their son could train at Tottenham for the next 18 months until he was 14 and then, if the situation remained the same, Dickie promised Tottenham wouldn't stand in his way if United wanted him.

Do you know who that lad was? Of course David Beckham. The lad really knew what he wanted and as everyone now knows, he hasn't changed.

I was quite fortunate with the scouting, as only within about three weeks of being taken on I was lucky enough to get Johnny Sutton, the brother of Chris Sutton the one-time Norwich, Blackburn, Chelsea & Celtic striker signed on for Tottenham, John Moncur coming up to Norfolk to do the signing. When I say lucky, I was watching a youth game at Norwich City's training ground and during half time I heard Danny Mills, the one-time Norwich, Leeds & Man City full back's father, telling somebody that Chris's father Mike, who has sadly just passed away with altzimers whilst I am writing this and who was a highly respected school teacher in Norwich, wasn't at all happy with the way his son Chris's transfer from Norwich to Blackburn had been handled by Norwich City, as Mike had represented his son Chris on his transfer from Norwich to Blackburn acting in effect as Chris's agent, he being angry that he allegedly didn't get the emolument from it that he should have from Robert Chase the then Norwich Chairman even though any that was due would have been far less than any agent would have received. Consequently, there was no way Mike would have let Johnny go to Norwich especially given that the general opinion was that Johnny was a far better footballer than Chris was at the same age. So I went to the next Norfolk County schools game with the intention of 'bumping into Mike,' to see whether he'd fancy Johnny coming to Tottenham, which he jumped at the chance of.

Actually, Johnny Sutton was a really talented footballer. He scored around 30 goals every season from the age of 14 right up to 17 when he signed youth academy forms and play for Spurs reserves, only to incur a sudden growth spurt which made him lose half a yard of pace in the box, which was essential in his ability to score the number of goals he did each season. Eventually, like his brother, he turned into a 'gangly' centre forward and Tottenham let him go, where after playing for a number of clubs in England, he has ended up playing in Scotland which is a shame, as he was an accomplished cricketer and could have easily made it in that sport as well. In fact I did see Johnny, Chris & Mike the father all play together in a match for Drayton Cricket Club up here in Norfolk once which would be a wonderful experience for any members of a family to do.

Around this time, with my days of 'competitive' football being over, I got involved in being the assistant manager for my local village team Felmingham in the North Norfolk League, as I did shortly after with my local market town team Alysham in the Anglian Combination League, also applying, albeit unsuccessfully, for the managers vacancy at Wroxham in the then as it was known Jewson League and Holt, again in the Anglian Combination League for which I had an interview. I have to say, the interview went quite well, albeit I and Holt F.C. mutually agreed that due to me not living in Norfolk for very long at the time, my lack of local football knowledge in terms of bringing in players into the club would be a disadvantage, which was completely true as that is what, unfortunately for me at the time, important at the level of football that they played in.

Whilst being the assistant manager at Felmingham, I invited my old team that I ran in Loughton, The Carpenter Arms, to come up to Norfolk to play a game, By this time they were all ageing, so they were pretty much a 'vets' team and I had to keep that in mind when getting our team together to play them, albeit I was hell bent on beating them. It was just after the '94 World Cup and I asked our lads to go out holding hands in one straight line like elephants do with their trunks and like the Brazilian's did in the World Cup Final of that year with the response being, especially them being hardened Norfolk lads, "What do ya think we are a bunch of poofs?" And so it didn't happen, which I was deeply upset about especially as when we got on the pitch, our opponents were lining up in a 1-9-1 formation asking me if I liked their new system of playing. They did it, because they knew that I was a real stickler for team systems and formations, in fact, although I might say it myself, I played with three centre halves and wing backs back in the early 80s when I ran a team before the French did it in winning the 1984 European Nations Cup.

I was always thinking outside the box when it came to tactics, so much so, that when I was invited to help coach the Norfolk County Schools teams, because there'd been so many goals scored direct from free kicks taken just outside the box, I came up with the idea of confronting the opposition with putting our five tallest players on the goal line, the keeper on the edge of the six yard box in front of them and four or five in a wall ten yards from where the kick was to be taken saying "now score." It was questioned with what we should do if the kick was say 'chipped' into the area between the keeper and the ten yard wall, as there wouldn't be an offside situation because of the players on the line, to which I replied "Well just run out from the goal line and 'smother' the ball."

When I was helping with the coaching of the Norfolk U-14/15s/& 16s we would take them over to Holland where we would play teams of a similar age to ours, sometimes even the youth teams of say PSV Eindhoven. We played their U-16s in a game with their no.10 being instrumental in controlling it. We gave away a free kick just to the left of the goal just outside the box. Their no. 10 couldn't wait to get to the ball to place it on the grass to go for the 'glory goal' except when he looked up, he saw our players within the aforementioned positioned formation with the five players on the line. He looked over to his coach who was standing next to me and my colleague. Their coach looked at me and then back to his player only to just shrug his shoulders as he had no answer to it. I also suggested this once to a top coach at Tottenham, at the same time asking why, when the opposition got a free kick say out near the touchline half way between the half way line and level with the penalty area, did our defenders being positioned in a line on the edge of our box retreat putting themselves on the back foot and on their heels and putting pressure on the keeper? I said to him, why not walk forward further as the kicker is taking the steps to take the kick so as to play their players offside.

I went onto say to him "If you're on your heels in any sport let alone football you're, excuse the pun, 'snookered,' as in being on the ropes in boxing and on the baseline in tennis, you've got to play on your toes not your heels."

He didn't really know what to say, except to come out with some crap about the modern day footballs being lighter, so much so that they swerve all over the place. Really?

As time went on, my scouting for the club got more and more difficult being somewhat remote in East Anglia. As I said previously, I was lucky with the John Sutton signing but I would never recommend a lad to the club unless I thought he had a very good chance of making it, at least with regards to signing youth forms. I thought it would be unfair on the parents for them to have to travel the four hours or so to take a lad backwards and forwards to London for training, even though there were no rules in place at the time for lads to have to make a certain number of visits to train with a club, so a club wouldn't care if he only in effect turned up for games if he was that good. Soon rules were put in place, such as a lad having to attend training at least three times a week and travelling down on a Sunday for a game and also, with any lads attending training sessions having to be within 90 minutes of any given clubs training facilities. There was one lad who came highly recommended to me by an ex-Norwich player, the lad being a 'striker' by the name of Jody Peacher. Jody, being 13/14 years of age and had been with Norwich City's youth team previously. In the 18 months or so since he had been released, he'd improved considerably and really looked as though he had immense potential when I went to see him play for his local junior side. Norwich wanted him back but his parents refused to let him return saying how badly he was treated when he was released. By their own admission, they didn't know much about football and left any real decision making with regards to the lads future with the guy who ran his Sunday morning junior team, who was more than keen to let him come to Tottenham. With the 90 minute rule in place, Colin Watts, who was head of Norwich City's Youth Academy at the time, went round to Jody's house on a Christmas Eve to ask his parents why Jody had been allowed to go down to Tottenham with the 90 minute ruling in place in mind. They replied by saying, they didn't care and emphasised that they weren't prepared to let him return to Norwich and if he wasn't allowed to go to Tottenham then they would pull him out and let him go back when he was 15 when the rule didn't apply, that is if Tottenham still wanted him.

Because of the situation, Norwich took Tottenham to a tribunal but before it took place, I suggested to John Moncur the Head of Academy at Tottenham, that he ask the tribunal what would be the situation if a lad didn't have a professional club within 90 minutes of his home and also to point out, that the ruling was unfair on the basis that some clubs were by the sea and by definition they were unfairly jeopardised given that they would only have half the diameter of an area to operate in. Evidently, Howard Wilkinson and Lawrie McMenemy were amongst the panel that were overseeing Norwich's protestation and I was told that Howard Wilkinson, when the two questions were put to them replied, "Oh, we didn't think of that."

You wouldn't admit to it if it was true would you?

Whilst coaching the Norfolk County Schools, we had a lad who was our U-16 captain who I sent down to the club who was taken on as a youth, his name being Greg Lake, no not him with Emerson & Palmer another one. We were over in Holland on one of the Easter trips going on a Monday and coming back Friday. Greg was due to play for Tottenham's U-16s against Chelsea at their training ground in Cobham the day after we were due to return home that being a Friday. On the Saturday, his parents were to take him down to Tottenham's training ground around 7.30a.m. to catch the coach but unfortunately on the Friday, the weather took a turn for the worse and the ferry that we were due to return on to Harwich was cancelled. Luckily for some reason, we were offered a return on a catamaran that left Rotterdam at almost Friday midnight arriving in Harwich around 6 on the Saturday morning. The problem was, customs at the port didn't open until 7.30 a.m. which left no time for Greg to get down to Cobham for the 10.30 kick off, having been picked up and taken down there by his mum and dad. Myself and the administrator of the Norfolk County Schools, who was on the trip with us, went to see the captain of the catamaran once we'd embarked on the boat to explain the circumstances, as we'd been given unusual dispensation for Greg to go on the trip to Holland by Tottenham. We'd already phoned his parents to get them to get to Harwich to meet us but at the time of doing so, we weren't aware of the customs not being open. Fortunately, the captain was sympathetic with the situation and I should imagine Greg's continued association with Tottenham. A lot of 'cloak & dagger' stuff went on that fortunately allowed Greg to bypass customs straight away when we docked and for his parents to whisk him off in time for the kick off.

Shortly after in 2004 Frank Arnesen, the ex-Dutch player was brought into Tottenham as a Director of Football. He almost overnight, sacked for whatever reason best known to him John

Moncur and John's right hand men, which personally I was really saddened about, as I had a lot of time and respect for John. When John was in charge of the academy, the scouts were always kitted out with track suits and padded winter coats and he allocated free tickets to the scouts in turn to watch the first team. In return for the tickets John gave me, because he had a penchant for them, I used to take down to him Cromer crabs wrapped in a polystyrene box with ice in it when I went down to the club for scout meetings

When I did go down to see a game with my free tickets, I'd often take in a youth game over in the training ground in Chigwell on the Saturday morning before the first team game. I remember once going to see the youth team play Arsenal with Graham Poll being the referee. It was a freezing cold morning and the ball went off the pitch for a throw-in right where I was standing. A fella next to me asked Graham "How long ref?" To which Graham replied, holding up his thumb and forefinger about an inch apart "What in this weather? About this long." I didn't know referees had a sense of humour.

I have to say, things were never the same at the club after Arnesen joined, the family feeling of how especially the youth set up was run by John Moncur just went out of the window, especially when the club moved its training headquarters to Hotspur Way, it became all very 'Blue-Chip' and impersonal. Now, if visitors enter Hotspur Way and they can get through the 'Fort Knox' procedure of gaining entrance, they have to go into the main entrance of the building with the players going through a separate entrance round the back. At Chigwell, you could sit and eat with the players but not at Hotspur Way. I remember on one occasion at Chigwell when Dimitar Berbatov signed for the club, he came and sat next to me to eat his breakfast with a copy of the Sun newspaper in his hand. On the back of it was a headline over a photo of Dimitar saying 'Nice but Dim' as used in the old Harry Enfield TV sketches. He said to me in broken English, "What does this mean?" I said to him "That's the British press for you, you'll just have to get used to it if not, and they see it gets to you, they'll do it all the time" for which he thanked me.

Mind you, Arnesen didn't care, he didn't hang around for long, after he changed things around he pissed off to Chelsea after a very short while.

As I said in the 'Warm Up' to the book, there's only two things that I haven't achieved in my life that I wanted to and that was to be a professional footballer and to live in Spain. I thought I'd get near to the latter when a few years ago, I heard a guy by the name of Ian Radford being interviewed by Paul Hawkesbee on Talksport one afternoon, who was the chief executive of Marbella Football Club, the club having recently been bought out by himself and a group of English businessmen. It was a very interesting interview, which made me wonder whether he'd be interested in acquiring lads that might not be quite good enough for the Premier League, having been released by their relative clubs but being good enough to play, as it was, in the 3rd Division of La Liga, which was the league that Marbella were playing in at the time. I had a friend who worked as a chef for my friend Peter Linane, who had a bar/restaurant by the name of Palms (more of that later), which was on the Marbella beach in the town's Puerto Maratimo. I telephoned her and asked her to get the address of the football club which she did and I wrote to Ian to see if he was interested in what I had to offer. This was in January and myself and my wife had booked flights to fly out to Malaga to stay with a friend who lived there in the March. I hadn't got a reply for a couple of weeks and almost forgot about it and then one day the phone rang which I picked up and said "Hello?" A voice at the other end enquired "Is that John?" To which I replied "Yes" to which he replied "This is Ian." Now I'd been talking to an Ian who was an architect that I'd had dealings with in my working life who sounded just like the caller, so I automatically said "Oh hello Ian" thinking it was him. The caller then said "You don't' know who this is do you?" I answered saying, yes Ian Garret." No no" he replied, its Ian Radford the Chief Executive of Marbella Football Club. My wife who was with me in the room, reckoned my bottom jaw dropped down to my waist, I was so shocked. Ian went onto say that he'd read my letter and that he was very interested in its contents and went on to ask if I could go out there and have a chat with him. I told him that my wife and I had booked the flights to go out in March about six weeks later but he didn't want to wait that long and asked us to go out as soon as possible with him paying the excess to change our flights and for us to stay in a hotel. Of course I agreed and we went a few days later. When we arrived and booked into the hotel, I went to meet Ian and the club's secretary in a bar/restaurant by the club's main entrance. The chat/interview went quite well, with Ian telling me that what they wanted to do is bring in at least one possibly two ex-U.K. Premier League players as they only had a striker by the name of Tommy Mooney, the one-time Watford player, in order to attract 'ex-pats' who lived on the Costa del Sol to the games. I think this was put to me as my initiation test to test my knowledge of playing personnel, so there and then I suggested two players, Dion Dublin and John Hartson. They said they'd had by coincidence spoken to John but he wasn't interested because of his fair skin not being conducive to the hot sun. As I left, I said that I would put some thought into a player who might be interested in what Ian had in mind on my return to England. They also asked me to return in a month or so to see a game and to go to the training ground to watch the team being coached by their coaches, which I did and was I have to say, very impressed by. Ian drove me back to the hotel in his beautiful leather upholstered BMW 7 Series convertible to meet up with my wife. When I walked into the room she said "You'll never guess who I saw in Zara's in the main Avenida just now? Only

Harry Redknapp and his wife Sandra." Now remember, this was in February in the middle of the English league season and he was manager of Portsmouth. I thought 'strange,' especially as Pompey were playing Preston in the cup the following Saturday. We went to Malaga Airport on the Thursday evening to come home and went into the bar to wait for our flight to be called. As I was ordering our drinks, who turned up and stood next to me, none other than Harry himself. It being a Thursday night, Tottenham were playing in the EUFA cup and for the want of just saying something to him I said "What are you doing here? Spurs are on the telly tonight playing in the EUFA Cup? " To which he replied surprisingly "Oh WE'LL win that easy." 'WE'll' I thought, was a strange thing to say. In the October of that year 2008, Harry was appointed manager of Tottenham and I bumped into him when I went down to the training ground in Chigwell for a scouts meeting. I was walking along a paved path that was only wide enough for one person to walk along, so submissively I moved to one side to let him through for which he thanked me. I said, "That's ok and by the way, we have met before" to which he replied, "I know the face, just remind me." I told him it was in Malaga Airport earlier in the year, to which he replied "Fuck me, so we did" and asked me what I was doing at the training ground. I said that I was the East Anglia Academy Scout and he said "Well done and keep up the good work."

When I returned home, I had a thought whilst driving along the A140 from Ipswich to Norwich of a player who I thought might be interested in playing for Marbella, Teddy Sheringham, wonder if he'd be interested? I knew John Moncur ,who gave me my appointment as a scout for Tottenham and who was now working for a football agency knew Teddy through his son John Moncur junior, who played with Teddy at West Ham. I explained to John what was going on and asked him to get in touch with Teddy and put it to him. John said that he would call him and if he was ok with it he would call me back with his number so that I could talk to him myself. He did agree, so John called me and gave me his number and I called him. Teddy liked the idea and gave me permission to let Ian the Marbella Chief Exec. get in touch with him and discuss it all.

I returned to Marbella to watch a game and to watch them training and whilst I was there, Ian told me that discussions didn't go as well with Teddy as he'd hoped, so it never materialised.

I'd come across Teddy some 12 years previously when he was playing for Spurs when my wife and I and our daughter Charley were walking across the pitches at Tottenham's then training ground at Mill Hill. Charley was only about 6 or 7 and was 'ambling' behind us. My wife turned around and told Charley to "keep up." As she did Teddy came passed us and said "Oh, is her name Charley? I've got a little boy named Charlie about the same age." Well my wife nearly sank to her knees with weakness, she thought he was so good looking and still does. I did see Teddy again many years later after the talks he had with Marbella F.C. I'd gone down to Loughton for the weekend to stay with a friend to watch a Spurs game on some 'hooky' TV Channel in a pub in Loughton, something I often used to do if a Spurs game wasn't on SKY, naughty I know but hey-ho. As I was walking back to Loughton Underground Station to go to Liverpool Street to catch the train to Norfolk, I stopped off in at fish n' chip shop in Loughton High Road. As I walked round the corner with my open bag of chips, I saw Teddy standing outside the popular Nu Bar that was often featured in The Only Way Is Essex. I went over to him and introduced myself as the guy who set up the conversation for him with Marbella F.C. for which he said he was grateful of and we had a chat about it, the only problem was I only ate a few chips as he and his drunken friends attacked my open bag of them like a flock of seagulls. Soon after, I arranged a three day trip with my wife and a friend and his wife to go to Granada and to take in an end of season game that

Marbella played them in, a game that Marbella had to win to secure promotion to La Liga 2. I'd arranged with Ian Radford to call him when I got there to meet him at the stadium entrance to pick up some 'free' tickets but as we arrived, he txt me to say that there was bad news, as by all accounts, he was banned from any Marbella games as the Spanish, because of Marbella's relative footballing success had come and virtually taken the club back under their control and that Ian was fighting them in court to get back the £750k plus that he and his business colleagues had invested in the club when buying it. Actually, we did pay to get in to see the game which was one of the most boring 0-0 draws I've ever seen.

I'd fallen in love with Marbella ever since myself and some friends in 1970/71, took a whole suitcase of record albums down there by such groups as The Who, The Stones and even some diverse as Frank Zappa and even Leo Sayer, we even took the first ever dartboard to be seen on the Costa del Sol, all at the request of my friend Keith Leffley who'd got a job down there in a bar. He was working in a bar in the old town off of the Orange Square called The Black Cat but the albums and dartboard were for a friend of his that ran a nearby bar by the name of La Tricycletta, a very popular bar there at the time. His friend was so grateful, my friends and I didn't buy drinks for the whole week that we were there.

I remember on my very first visit to Marbella to see my friend Keith, I met a gorgeous Belgian girl by the name of Sue. It was a bit of a 'holiday romance' I suppose, although I never did get my wicked way with her and I was really sad when I had to come home, whether I was sad that I wouldn't be seeing her anymore or because I had to leave Marbella I'm not sure. On the day I was to leave, I was with my friends in a bar in the Orange Square in Marbella, a bar that a Lebanese fella by the name of Freddie had waiting for a taxi to take us to the airport. As said, to say I was forlorn about leaving was an understatement and I was sitting at the end of the bar having my final San Miguel when a friend of the aforementioned Sue came in. She didn't see me at first so she asked one of my friends where I was and he pointed over to me. She came over and said "Sue wanted you to have this to remember her by." When I looked down it was a silver puzzle ring that I straight away put on the little finger of my left hand that I cherished for some time. When I returned to England, quite a while after I was playing for the earlier mentioned in the book Bill Bedford's Sunday morning team in the Waltham District League ostensibly made up of Hertfordshire teams. We were playing against a Hertfordshire village team 'managed/run' by the then Spurs winger Ralph Coates as he resided in the village. I was playing on the left wing on the same side of the pitch that Ralph was standing on on the half way line and about 15 minutes from the end of the game, as I ran past their right full back he pulled me back by the wrist of my left hand (not Ralph their full back) but I suppose what with sweat and the white oils that I used my hand to rub onto my legs before the game, his hand slid down mine to my fingers whereby he pulled of the ring given to me by the lovely Sue for keepsake. I was devastated and I spent the last 15 minutes of the game searching through the mud churned up pitch for the ring with the assistance of Ralph Coates all to the annoyance of my team mates and dear old Bill Bedford. In fact, a few weeks later, I bumped into Ralph again in the popular 'Room At The Top' club that was on top of Harrison's Furniture Store in Ilford one Thursday night where he was there with another Spurs player Phil Beal and Ralph asked me if I ever did find the ring which unfortunately I hadn't, so sad.

When my friend Keith left Tottenham and went down to Marbella it was pre-mobile days, so he used to write to me on a regular basis to keep me in touch with what was going on with him. In one letter, he said that he'd met a beautiful girl by the name of Leigh. He went on to say that he'd taken her to a bar in the Marbella old town called The International Bar more commonly known as Cozzi's, as owned by an East London guy by the name of Paul, Cozzi being his surname. In my mind's eye, I envisaged it being some salubrious bar with a barman in the top bar standing there in a white 'dickie' mixing cocktails with the restaurant area being in the downstairs level, albeit it being nothing of the sort. In his letter, Keith said he was sitting at the bar with his new lady, when a rather large gentleman came up to her and said that 'George' wanted to have a word, pointing to a fella sitting in the corner. When she and Keith turned, there in the corner was the mercurial George Best. It transpired that she and George had been an item for some time, albeit she dumped him when he started 'playing around. There's a surprise. George evidently asked her to go back with him, saying that if she did they could get engaged, which she declined and decided to stay with my friend, the fool, her not him. Myself and the gang of lads who Keith used to be a part of in Tottenham, started to go down there almost every opportunity, every Bank Holiday and for our two week annual holidays just to see him and enjoy the company of the beautiful girls that congregated there. On the first time we flew down there, we were introduced by Keith to the aforementioned Leigh where we witnessed the beauty of how he described her. As said, we took the first ever dartboard to be seen on the Costa del Sol down there along with the suitcase full of albums but on our arrival some guy asked me if we'd riven down or come by plane? I answered, " By plane" to which he replied "You couldn't have been stopped by customs then, if so, the stuff would have been confiscated and you would have ended up in a cell for at least a night." Phew that was lucky then, as it was in the reign of Franco and we didn't realise how the regime operated. I remember also, when we went down there at Easter everywhere was shut, there were no bars open we were just lucky that our friend Keith had the keys to the bar where he worked. I remember one time being up on the first floor balcony of the bar watching the effigy of Christ being carried along below us on a cross in a procession with this haunting beat of a drummer leading it, it was eerie.

One afternoon, a guy our friend Keith new took six of us, boys and girls down to the newly opened Puerto Banus in his 2CV Citroen, also known as a Deux Chevaux I believe. The thing was rolling from side to side and suddenly a couple of outboard police motorcyclists appeared next to us frantically waving us over to the side of the road. Obviously we thought we were going to be done for driving dangerously or something but alas no, they were just pushing us over to the side of the road to enable a cavalcade of grey blacked out windowed Mercedes to go past. We didn't think anymore of it but when we got to the port we noticed a naval frigate moored just outside of it. By all accounts, the waters in the port were too shallow for the ship to go in so it had to stay outside. The word soon got round that it was General Franco on board and later in the evening, we saw him go through the main Avenida in Marbella in one of the Mercedes that we were pushed over for earlier in the day so that they could pass us. I must say, it was an amazing scene to see the locals kneeling down bowing to him in awe, with he having his window half way down waving to his 'subjects I suppose you would call them. At least I can say I saw him.

One time when we were down there, there was a 24 hour rock concert held at the newly opened bullring just up at the back of Puerta Banus. There were hundreds and hundreds of hippy type people converging on Marbella for the weekend, some just to be there with others actually paying to see the likes of Lou Reed and his Velvet Underground and The Creedence Clearwater Revival. Paul Cozzi opened up the bar on the roof terrace of his International Bar for his close friends so that they wouldn't have to mingle with all the hippies that flooded into

Marbella and drank downstairs, we being invited as our friend Keith was well indoctrinated into the Marbella way of life by now and had become good friends with Paul. I was by the roof bar that was approxiamately 2 metres square, having my back to the bar leaning on my elbows talking to my friend Fudgie, who was opposite facing me with us chatting up two girls that were either side of us. Fudgie said to me "Your friends behind you over there" nodding to where I was to look. Now Fudgie didn't know sod all about football, so I was surprised when I looked round to see only George Best leaning on the bar having a drink on his own. George at the time, was living in Marbella in an apartment in the Skol, as was James Hunt who had a club named Oscars which James named after his beloved Alsatian dog and as was too Sean Connery, who lived behind a great little restaurant named El Refugio which was on the road just behind Marbella that led up to Monda and Coin up in the mountains. In fact you always knew when Sean Connery was at home, which was a small like castle that you could see across the valley from El Refugio as he would raise his Scottish flag to show that he was in residence. El Refugio, was owned around 1984 by a guy who was a very good footballer whose name I can't remember who at one time played for the Belgian club Anderlecht, who Spurs had beaten a few months earlier in the final of the EUFA Cup which he didn't like me reminding him of when I and my wife visited the restaurant a couple of times whilst we were on holiday just after the final had been played . The restaurant was very popular with many of the footballers that used to have properties in Marbella or were visiting it, in fact I remember seeing Bobby Moncur the one time Newcastle player in there once.

Back on the roof terrace of Cozzi's, George's and my eyes sort of met as I turned around, with him saying to me in his deep Irish brogue "You alright?" To which I answered "Yes thank you George and yourself?" Funnily enough, we weren't dissimilar, me being in my 20s and very slim with long dark hair. So 'what's a boy to do,' I had a choice of spending the evening and hopefully the night with one of the gorgeous girls that Fudgie and I were 'chatting up' or George Best? Sorry George!

While I was down in Marbella once it was suggested by one of Keith's friends, that I should bang on the door of Marbella Football Club and offer my services and have a trial for them but at the time I had a pensionable job with BT, or the Post office as it was still known at the time and I was regularly playing for Leyton in the Athenian League and anyway, Marbella football club wasn't like it was when I went to speak to them about the scouting all those years later. That said, I did play in a game down there in the early/mid 80s. My friend Peter, who had Palms in Marbella, organised a game between what he called The Marbella All Bars against RAF Gibraltar. I was down there with my wife on holiday at the time and he asked if I would play. The RAF team arrived in a luxury coach kitted out in their pristine blue & claret kit. We had nothing like that, we played topless albeit in dark blue shorts and white socks that Peter dragged up from somewhere. We'd only got to four minutes into the game when yours truly opened the scoring with a header, something that I was never renowned for, heading I mean, with Peter bemoaning the fact that he would never hear the end of it from me. I ended the game the worse for wear drink wise, as every time I went over to take a corner a spectator, of which there were many, gave me a bottle of San Miguel to take a swig out of. The RAF boys were much fitter than us and more suited to the cinder type pitch that we played on and with about 15 minutes to go they were leading 3-1. Peter thought "Right I've had enough of this" and put all of the players that he had at his disposal onto the pitch at the same time,14 or 15 of us and the RAF still managed to score, running out 4-1 winners. It was a great afternoon though and we all, the RAF boys as well ended up down at Peter's bar drinking. I was sitting on the beach having a beer when Peter brought a guy over to me and said "Here he is." It turned out he was a reporter for the local English SUR newspaper and proceeded to interview me about my goal, in fact I still have a copy of the paper to this day.

As said, Peter had the bar 'Palms' and opened it originally with three of his friends who had been his work colleagues at a company in Shoreditch in London namely City Electrical. They were working there just at the right time to earn good money, as it was the time that office workers were going over to electronic typewriters from the old conventional type. I met Peter through a girl that my wife and I knew Jan, as they were an item at the time, it helping that he and his brother Baz and his dad were all massive Spurs fans, sadly though, his dad died of a heart attack at home during half-time watching the 1991 F.A. Cup semi-final when Gascoigne scored that wonder free-kick. I wondered if his dad ever did know the final score 3-1 to Tottenham, I hope so. Jan invited myself and my wife to one of Peter's birthdays being held in near to where he worked the Spread Eagle Pub, situated in Kingsland Road in Shoreditch owned by the one-time bantam & featherweight boxer Vic Andretti. The three of us, Jan, my wife and I arrived at the pub before Peter and his friends finished work but soon after they came in, with Peter coming up to me saying "I've got some bad news for you Johnny." Peter didn't know me that well and definitely didn't know my family, which made me wonder why he had 'bad news' for me?

What he did know, was of my desire at some stage to live in Marbella and then informed me, just to wind me up as much as anything, that he and three of his friends had bought a bar there with, for the most part, the money that they'd accrued selling electronic typewriters at just the right time. I think I responded by saying something like, "You jammy bastard," in an endearing way of course.

The idea, because of the uncertainty as to what money they would make, at least during the early stage of having the business, was that Peter and his friend John would go out there to 'run it' with the other two guys being 'sleeping partners' staying in England. Peter and John were really enjoying themselves socially, whilst at the same time doing very well financially.

I have to say, Peter played a big part in making the bar a success, as he was a tall red-haired effervescent type of guy with a great personality, that was instrumental in many ex-pats frequenting the place on a regular basis and by definition of them living in Marbella spending a considerable amount of money in there. I remember one-time when we were on holiday down there, we arranged to meet a friend of mine who was my mechanic in London and his wife who were also holidaying down there at the same time. We met in Puerta Banus and after we'd spent a couple of hours with them drinking in Sinatra's, we suggested that we should go back to Peter's so that they could meet him and have a nightcap. We arrived there about midnight and although all the lights were on, there was no-one to be seen not on either side of the bar, it was like the Marie Celeste. Then after a short while, Peter appeared on the beach which the bar was right adjacent to with a friend of his by the name of Murray Feeley, a lovely guy who I've since befriended, with about twenty people behind them doing the conga.

We stayed a lot longer than we intended, in fact as daylight broke around 6 o'clock, there was a bang on the shutters that Peter had pulled down to keep the noise down. As he bent down to lift them up, there were two pairs of large black boots and as he pushed the shutters up further he exposed the wearers of said boots, two patrolling policemen who said to Peter knowing him "Don't you think you ought to go home now."

After some time one of the sleeping partners Andrew, decided he'd had enough of working in England and decided he would have 'a piece of the action' down on the Costa del Sol. He understood that he couldn't go down there and take money out of the business, even if he did spend time working in the bar, which by this time had turned into a restaurant/bar doing as I said very well. After about six or so months, Andrew, whether it was because of his funds running out or for some other reason decided he would have to return to England. Now Andrew, was a great raconteur and at the same time a bit of a 'Walter Mitty' character, having the ability to tell many anecdotal stories some 'tongue in cheek' but I can only imagine this was true as Peter was there at the time.

It turns out that Peter, was sweeping out the bar at about 11a.m. one morning when Freddie Foremen, who was a well known alleged criminal came into it with another guy. Peter, knowing who Freddie was, said that the bar wasn't yet open but Freddie replied that he wasn't there for a drink he was looking for a guy named Andrew that he knew had some relationship with the bar. Peter asked Freddie why he wanted to see him, with Freddie telling Peter that " Andrew had been 'playing around' with his friend's wife," pointing to the chap next to him. Peter responded by saying that Andrew had gone back to England the previous week and he was sorry but "he wasn't his brothers keeper," to which Freddie responded to by saying "You're not telling me porkies, are you Peter?" To which Peter replied "Of course not Freddie," knowing full well of what might have happened to him if he did and luckily Freddie and his pal left albeit muttering something like "You need to be careful who you mix with" or something similar.

As said, Andrew was back in England staying with his parents in Nottingham, although he owned a house in Clapham that he let his sister live in. One Saturday around noon, he received a phone call with the caller saying "Is that Andrew?" To which he replied in the affirmative. The caller then went onto say "I hear you've been playing around with my wife" mentioning her name, to which Andrew replied "I didn't know that she was married." The fella then suggested to Andrew that they should meet in London from where he was calling. Andrew said that he would be down in London in two weeks time to see his beloved Nottingham Forest take on Arsenal at the Highbury Stadium, their home ground at the time and asked if he could meet him then. The caller then said "Andrew, I don't think you understand. If I tell you that I am in the hallway of a house in Clapham, with a young lady sitting on the stairs who I believe is your sister, do you think you could get down today? How he found her I never did find out. Andrew then went onto say that he didn't have a car, which he didn't, only for the caller to say that there were trains running from Nottingham to London and suggested that if he caught the 2 o'clock he would arrive at Kings Cross at 4 where he would be waiting for him. Andrew had no choice but to go but first asked how he would recognise him, for the caller to say that he would be outside the station in a maroon convertible Rolls Royse Corniche, which he was. When Andrew arrived the fella took him round to a local Kings Cross pub but nothing really happened, I just think the fella wanted to let Andrew know that he knew, as the fella and his wife weren't really an item anymore, in fact a weird thing happened a little later. The fella's wife was besotted with Andrew and she suffered over it mentally and the story goes that the fella offered Andrew a quarter of a million pound for him to buy a house and let her move in with him so he could look after her but by this time, Andrew had met another lady and was about to get engaged which complicated matters further but luckily nothing ever came of it allowing Andrew to continue with his relationship which to this day he is happy in, with a couple of children.

As said, Andrew was a great story teller and I hope this is true. He once told me whilst he was living in Nottingham, he was listening to a commentary of Notts County playing against someone. They had a winger by the name of John Chiedozie, who later actually played for Tottenham amongst other teams. Andrew said, the commentator got rather excited when Chiedozie was running down the wing and got away from a couple of defenders and only had the keeper to beat. He reckoned the commentator said something like "It's Chiedoze, he's gone past one defender, now another and he's only got the keeper to beat, he shoots and he's hit the 'fookin' bar" never to be heard on the radio again.

The 80s was a great time to be on the Costa Del Sol. I remember going to Joe's Bar in Puerto Banus at the time, seeing the likes of Frank Worthington and Paul Walsh in there both in fact being dressed in leather suits, Frank's being black with long leather trousers and Paul's being beige albeit with leather shorts. Actually I have to say, Frank Worthington was the best centre-forward that England never had in the same way that as I've said earlier Ledley King was the best centre half that England never had, in my opinion of course. There was also, half way between Puerto Banus & the town of Marbella backing onto the beach Tony Dalli's restaurant, a 50-50 business partnership comprising of Tony Dalli and Jimmy Tarbuck. I remember our table being serenaded one night by the wonderful operatic voice of Tony Dalli singing More Than Ever, or to give it its real title 'O Sole Mio.' There was also another 'great' Italian restaurant we would frequent in Marbella itself, by the name of Mamma Mia's, owned by a real cool Italian dude that my wife enjoyed going to just because of him.

I, my friend Guy and my wife, went on holiday down there together in the 80s, Guy coming with us on his own as he'd split with his wife after we'd paid for it. We caught the bus from Marbella to Puerto Banus and decided to walk back the six or so miles along the beach. As we were walking along on the edge of the beach where it met the sea, we, that being I, Guy and my wife in that order passed a popular beach drinking venue called 'Frank's' noticing that Frank Bruno was sitting at the bar although it wasn't he who owned it. Guy and I also noticed that there was a young lady in our line of site of Frank Bruno who was rubbing sun cream into her well endowed breasts. So enamoured was I with the site of this, not looking where I was going, I walked straight into a kiddie's sand castle that stood about a half metre high with flags stuck into the top that the kiddies father had obviously help him build. I sought of stopped myself from actually walking into it but because Guy behind me was still transfixed in the direction of the aforementioned lady, he walked straight into the back of me making me fall forward right on top of said sand castle which almost flattened it which brought great laughter and enjoyment to all those on the sun lounges around the bar and Frank Bruno and of course my wife, who said to me and Guy. "That will teach you." That said the kiddie's father wasn't at all happy.

As I said earlier in the book, the only two regrets that I have in life were not being a professional footballer and not living in Spain, albeit I've spent so much time there over the years, not least because I've been able to visit my friend Terry who has been a friend for some almost 60 years who lives down on the Costa del Sol, that I almost feel I have.

It's something I really enjoy staying in his finca up in the hills above Marbella, swimming in his pool, drinking his one euro ninety eight cents beautiful wine that we get from the local Supermercado, playing his 1950's albums and just generally talking shite. Why do I need to go anywhere else for a holiday when I know for definite that I'm going to enjoy myself.

Back to the present, in terms of the scouting. I suppose I didn't get as many lads down to the club from Norfolk as I was expected to, that said, I probably set my standards too high, notwithstanding that if I didn't think a lad had an exceptional chance of making it if, as I've said previously, I didn't think it fair on the parents to get a lad down to training three times a week and to play at the weekend which was the case when the rules got stricter as to what was required.

Not only that, as is the way with modern day marriages and relationships, more and more seem to fail with the parents breaking up and if the mother is awarded the custody of the children, it's not easy for her to transport a lad that may have potential to training whilst leaving his siblings at home. This is a problem, there are so many lads out there that have the ability to make it only for them not to get the opportunity because of the circumstances they find themselves in.

A prime example of this, was with a lad I saw playing for the Norfolk County Schools side, a black lad, the first black lad to represent the county since Dale Gordon many years before. He was 15 at the time and reminded me of a young Valencia of Manchester United when he first came to England and played on the right wing. He even had a similar physique to him which he would show off when he was dressed in black trousers and a black sleeveless vest, he looked a real cool dude. For the sake of his and his family's privacy I'll just refer to him by his christian name Danny. He lived with his mother who was from the east end of London originally and other siblings. There were six of them all in all, I'm not certain that they were all brothers and sisters but his mum looked after all of them as he didn't have a father. There was no way his mum could have taken him down to Tottenham, so for the first game he had for the club my wife and I got up at 5.30. on a Sunday morning to go and pick him up and take him down to Forty Hill where the youth used to play their games before it was converted into Hotspur Way.

When we arrived, I introduced him to one of the coaches who told him to go and get changed but as he went to go into the dressing room he took off his jacket only to unveil an Arsenal shirt, the bugger. I was waiting outside the dressing room talking to someone when one of the coaches asked me if 'Danny' had filled in a medical questionnaire, something that I didn't know had to be done. So I went into the dressing room questionnaire in hand, when a club administrator came in and asked me what I was doing in there with 'Danny' on my own which evidently wasn't allowed. He said it so aggressively, I told him to fucking make his mind up as, as I said to him, a coach had sent me in there to fill in the questionnaire as he couldn't trial without it and now you're telling me I can't be in here on my own with him, bloody red tape. As we commenced the form filling, the first part of it was about his father and mother with the question asking about the state of his father's health. Unfortunately, Danny told me that his father had had a heart attack to which I replied "Is he ok now?" To which Danny replied "No he died when he had it." I didn't know what to say to the poor kid, hence his mother living on her own.

Anyway he played and Tottenham won 5-1 with him really impressing. He was invited to go back the following week but before he could, we had to get the signatures of two custodians of his. His mother was obviously one and she suggested that his 'uncle,' who lived in Norwich, should be the other, he living on what was called The Larkman Estate, which was one of those areas housing the 'rough' type of person that every city has. I drove round there in my Golf GTI that I had at the time and left it, reluctantly outside the block of flats in which he lived on the ground floor. As I locked the car and walked away from it, looking at it over my shoulder thinking the wheels might be removed Danny's 'uncle' came to the door and welcomed me in saying, "Don't worry about the car John, nothing will happen to it whilst you're with me." He was a rather big Rastafarian type of gentleman and invited me to sit down and proceeded to roll a joint asking me if I wished to partake, which obviously I declined, or did I?. We got talking and as luck had it, he started telling me about a girl friend that he once had who was the mother of his daughter who lived in Wood Green, North London just up the road from White Hart Lane and that he would be able to take 'Danny' down to Tottenham for training and any games that he needed to play in so that he could see his daughter more, which was handy. 'Danny' played in two more games which Tottenham won very convincingly 8-1 and 9-0, the latter being against MK Dons, whereby in a patronising kind of way. Tottenham kept taking off one lad every 5 minutes 15 minutes from the end so as to, in their minds, even the game up. Danny was well liked by the other lads in the team, in fact he did show me the txts he was getting especially from the other black lads, sending messages like "Good to see you bro, looking forward to seeing ya next week."

After the 9-0 victory, I spoke to Chris Ramsey, a lovely guy who was coach of the U-16s of which Danny was a part of and asked him what he was going to do about him. Chris said he wasn't sure, he said that he was six months behind the other lads and that if he had been there at the start of the season he would have been ok but Chris was uncertain about him. I told Chris that Danny was a quick learner but the decision was finally made not to take him on, the poor sod. I still maintain it was Tottenham's loss, as he went out to the states just after and played out there.

Just another couple of quick stories about the scouting of which there were many. I was asked once to 'run the rule' over Wilfred Zaha whilst playing for Palace at Norwich when he was 14. He obviously had something about him but I told Tottenham that the lad who looked more impressive was their lad on the other wing, Bolasie.

Also, there is a guy who lives in a market town near me, the town being named Aylsham and he is a frequent visitor to Scotland. He's a big Spurs fan but used to watch Hamilton Academicals whenever he went up there, which he adopted as his second team. He once came back and knowing that I represented Tottenham he handed me a piece of paper with the names of James McArthur and James McCarthy on it, saying "Get Tottenham to have a look at these two." As we all know, they've both done quite well for themselves in the PL but when I told Tottenham about them, they said they were aware of them but not quite what they were looking for, which may be true. Incidentally, the guy mentioned above once told me that his '15 minutes of fame' is that it was his great grandfather that designed the 'cockerel' on the original Spurs shirts.

When I used to go down to Chigwell for scouts meetings, I used to stay in a friends house that backed on to a pub by the name of The Foresters that overlooked Epping Forest in Loughton. A number of years ago, I got introduced to a policeman, a Scotsman who was living near Loughton. Evidently he hadn't been a bad player himself, having played for amongst other Scottish teams, St. Johnstone and had been manager of Stanstead. He said I should get Tottenham to look at his nephew, who was with Inverness Caledonian Thistle at the time, a lad by the name of Ryan Christie who is now a regular in the Celtic team, another that I did recommend but alas was deemed not good enough for the club.

As said, it took me to move to Norfolk to be appointed as a scout for the club, which was pretty much part-time and I must admit I would have loved to have been a scout on full-time basis perhaps even getting some kind of promotion higher up the ladder but that would have only happened if I'd stayed in London I guess. As time went on, it was getting more and more difficult to find lads in East Anglia that had the potential of making it into professional football, especially in comparison to the lads of the same age that the club were now bringing in from Europe and even further afield, making the competition far greater than it even was. In fact, in the end, all I was doing was giving second opinions on lads that had been recommended by a scout in other parts of the country. For example, if a Midland Spurs scout would have seen a lad playing for say Birmingham City or West Brom, then Tottenham would find out when whatever club it was they were playing in my area, Norwich or Ipswich and ask me to go along and have a look so as to give a second opinion, which I suppose was a bit of a back-handed compliment. The problem was, if I thought the lad could 'cut the mustard' all I would get out of it was my mileage expenses, in fact, it would be the scout who initially saw him who would be the one who received the financial emolument. This was the thing with scouting, we were all on expenses/mileage, so unless you were successful in getting a lad signed on into the academy whereby the financial rewards were relatively good if a lad progressed through the ranks to be signed as a professional, financially you wouldn't gain from it, nobody did it for the money, it was all done for the 'love of the club' in the hope that you could make the club successful in some way, well at least it was with me. That said, I did stand up at a meeting to suggest that if a player was sold for a considerable amount of money, then the scout who brought him in should get a percentage of the transfer fee, even if it was for say 1 or 2 per cent, which was completely pooh-poohed! Actually, what made me suggest it, was when Sol Campbell was about to go to Arsenal and there was talk of him going for around £18m at the time, with the percentage being a nice little earner for the scout who brought him to the club, albeit as we now all know, Campbell waited for his contract to expire so that he could walk for nothing in the end.

When I reached the ripe old age of 72, I decided that I'd had enough of going over a park or school playing field on a freezing cold winter's Saturday or Sunday morning in the hope of finding the next Lionel Messi, I just couldn't do it anymore

So I requested a chat with my club co-ordinator who said "So what do you want to do now then, surely having been scouting for the club for 26 years you don't want to just sever your relationship with them completely do you?" I answered "no," so we agreed that I could still continue my association with the club not least because of my continued connection with the Norfolk County Schools by me still going to see their games, metaphorically with my Spurs hat on, so that I would continue to let the club know of any potential lads that were worth a look at whether it be the Norfolk lads or other lads in the opposition from other counties

By coincidence around this time, I'd become quite friendly with Colin Watts who had been Head of Norwich City's Academy even though he was instrumental in taking Tottenham to the tribunal over the issue with me taking that lad Jody Peacher down to the club, that lived in Norwich that I wrote about earlier in the book. Colin got in touch with me, as Norwich had a vacancy for a scout, to ask if I'd be interested in going for an interview, as he thought it would be ideal for me living in the area. I was reluctant to go as I questioned myself as to whether I could scout for Norwich with the same fervour and enthusiasm as I'd done for Tottenham but after giving it some thought, I agreed to go along and see what they had to offer. As the day of the interview got nearer, I was hoping more and more that I would be successful in being appointed for the position but whilst I was being interviewed, I got the impression that those interviewing me were more interested in how Tottenham did things rather than how I would do them, in fact I did ask the question during it, "Excuse me, are you interviewing me or Tottenham Hotspur?". However, alas, it wasn't to be, having got down to the last three, I was told later by someone that my age had gone against me.

So that was my scouting days over really, 26 plus years for Tottenham and no gold watch, the only thing I got out of it was an invitation to attend the opening of the new wonderful Tottenham Hotspur Stadium given to me by the wonderful hard working Donna Cullen, Daniel Levy's 'right hand lady.'

A rather sad way to end my involvement in football I suppose after all those years.

As I said early doors and 'banged on about' in the beginning of the book, it's the 'grass roots of football' where the game started that we shouldn't forget. That said, I've watched a lot of professional football over the years mainly because of where I was brought up very near to White Hart Lane but as I'm coming to the end of writing this book, my 'beloved' Spurs are in turmoil having supposedly potential managers turning down the opportunity of managing us having sacked Jose Mourinho.

Perhaps I'm being too idealistic, as I am in wanting to see performance related players salaries but a part of me would like to see 'proper' Tottenham people involved in the set-up of running the club as we do have currently, in addition to the owners, Ryan Mason & Ledley King on the coaching side and the likes of Cliff Jones, Martin Chivers & Gary Mabbutt as matchday ambassadors. Surely there must be room for others e.g. Glenn Hoddle & Graham Roberts, people who would represent the club in some capacity or another with the club in their heart, as I'd like to think I did throughout my 26 years of scouting for the club.

We've now got the wonderful stadium that is a contrast between the old and new of the area, that sits looking over Tottenham like a space ship that has just landed, like a cathedral that the residents can look up to worship like the Catalans of Barcelona do with their Nou Camp Stadium. We should have the scouting capability to find amongst the thousands and thousands of lads living in and around the Tottenham area good enough and proud enough to wear the colours to represent the club in the future, so that we don't have to spend unnecessary millions of pounds on what turn out to be mediocre players.

Unfortunately I can't see it happening, we will have to continue to bring in managers/coaches probably from overseas just to keep up our high-profile image.

That said, I do have a certain amount of sympathy with Daniel Levy with regards to the European Super league debacle. He was 'dammed if he did and dammed if he didn't' involve us in the setting up of it, as who would have known what would have happened if it had gone ahead without us in it, especially with the stadium in mind.

To my mind, we're only delaying the inevitability of it raising its head again as the world in a travelling sense is forever decreasing in size.

At this juncture I just want to say, I and all Spurs fans must love our club Tottenham Hotspur and if we cut ourselves, our blood would come out blue and we must be 'true' fans as we certainly aren't 'glory hunters,' most certainly those that started supporting the club since the early 70s not like supporters of the other big so-called six clubs.

That said at times and I know it's easy for me to say because I'm not and without being patronising, I would love to be a Leyton Orient fan whereby the fans expectations aren't so high. I suppose it's like the higher up you are expectation wise, it hurts more when you've a longer way to fall and believe me, I've fallen quite a lot and often being a Spurs fan with a lot of bruises to prove it.

Still. I still have the wonderful memories of what great fun 'football' has given me, memories which nobody can take away from me that I've recollected by being able to write this book and on that note, I'd like to give a mention and thanks to all those named and unknowingly contributed to the book and my life, which for the most part has made it fun and the Tottenham Hotspur players over the years that I have seen that have made the hairs on the back of my neck stand up and in later years, when all seating stadiums came into play, made me get off my seat when they were 'running at the opposition with the ball at their feet,' the likes of Johnny White, Jimmy Greaves, Cliff Jones, Martin Chivers (on a good day), Ricky Villa in that memorable F.A. Cup replay, Paul Gascoigne, David Ginola, Gareth Bale, Harry Kane and Son Heung-Min, as he did v Burnley in 2020 in our 5-0 victory at The Lane and possibly controversially, Tanguy N'dombele who I just love to watch and Chrissy Waddle, who once said himself, "I knew when I was having a good game, when I was running down the wing and I could hear all the seats 'clacking' as the fans would get off them to stand up and cheer me on." Obviously there were other 'Great' technically gifted 'touch' players that have blessed the club e.g. Blanchflower, Hoddle, Ardiles, Berbatov, Modric and Rafael van der Vaart and others for which I apologise by excluding them but the former were the ones who really excited me.

ADDED ON TIME

So that is me, the final whistle has blown, only football wise thank God and now that I've finished the book, I can concentrate on my next mission in life, that is to convert my wonderful four year old grandson Oscar into being a Spurs fan, as his dad has commandeered him into being a Gooner as is he, albeit I think my grandson is somewhat confused as he has a signed autograph to him personally by Harry Kane in his bedroom.

Because my wife kept having a go about me not getting any exercise, as I spend pretty much all my time sitting in front of my laptop, I decided I would take up 'walking football' that took place every Wednesday morning in an adjoining village to mine. To my surprise, I could still bang the goals in, they even asked me to represent them in an over 60s national competition even though I was 72 by then but then I started to get a pain in my hip, something I always dreaded in the event I might have to have a hip operation. But the pain went around my buttocks and down to my legs and after going for an MRI scan, it was diagnosed that, probably due to all the football that I'd played over the years, my discs were worn and they were pushing down onto my nervous system, a problem it seems that I've just got to put up with as there doesn't seem to be a cure.

So I thought "That's it then, no participation, no scouting, there isn't even the 'Foul' magazine to read that took a cynical view of football back in the 70s, just observation of the game either on TV or to watch my local side Aylsham in the East Anglia Combination League. That said, that isn't happening as I write this due to the coronavirus pandemic. As some-one said on the radio the other day, "Football may have come back to some degree professional wise but it won't completely until we can play 5 a-sides in the gym or with our team mates over the park" which is true and what this book is really trying to say and is all about.

But wait a minute, there's a twist to all of this.

I sometimes go to a quintessential quaint Norfolk pub by the name of the Rose and Crown in a village called Frettenham, to have a drink once a month with a friend of mine who lives there having moved from the village where I live. A couple of years ago, I was in there talking football with my friend, when one of the locals who overheard us talking said, "If you're a Spurs fan, you shouldn't be drinking in here, you should be drinking in a pub two miles down the road, the publican in there is a massive Spurs fan." So one Friday afternoon on the way back home from Norwich where I'd been shopping, I called into the pub The Longe Arms. It was around 3 in the afternoon and when I looked around there was a 'White Hart Lane N.17' metal street sign on a ceiling wooden beam and a signed Harry Kane framed shirt on the wall. There was only the publican in there 'Oggie' it turned out was his name, who by all accounts similar to myself, moved up from North London, Stamford Hill for, contrary to what Dr. Johnson said ("If you're fed up with London you're fed up with life") a better quality and pace of life. I cut the ice by saying, "It's a pity he's not playing tomorrow (Saturday)." Pointing to the framed shirt of Harry Kane, as Tottenham were playing Man U up at Old Trafford but he'd just got injured. Oggie asked me if I was fan, to which I took the opportunity of telling him that my involvement was a bit more than that and that I'd been a scout for them for 26 years which he was very interested in.

As it turned out 'Oggie,' wasn't just any old 'Oggie,' he is Harry Kane's uncle and because of the friendship that we've since formed, he took me to Leicester not long after we made our acquaintance where he introduced me to Harry's dad Pat and brother Charlie and has taken me and my wife since to the new stadium to watch some games in Harry's private box for which we are both most grateful and especially, as that's where my wife and I got Harry to sign that photograph personally to my grandson.

On top of that, Oggie and I have formed the Norfolk branch of the Spurs Supporters Club, or the 'TIN ARMY' (Tottenham In Norfolk) as we prefer to call it, with yours truly being Chairman, so all is not lost with my involvement in football after all and hopefully, I will be able to retain my association with TOTTENHAM TILL I DIE.!